Feelings

Feelings

A course in conversational English for upper-intermediate and more advanced students

Adrian Doff and Christopher Jones

Cambridge University Press

Cambridge

London   New York   New Rochelle

Melbourne   Sydney

To Patrick and Stephanie Early

Published by the Press Syndicate of the University of Cambridge
The Pitt Building, Trumpington Street, Cambridge CB2 1RP
32 East 57th Street, New York, NY 10022, U.S.A.
296 Beaconsfield Parade, Middle Park, Melbourne 3206, Australia

First published 1980

Printed in Great Britain at
the Alden Press, Oxford

ISBN 0 521 21847 0 Student's Book
ISBN 0 521 21846 2 Teacher's Book
ISBN 0 521 21845 4 Cassette

Contents

Preface   vii
To the student   1

Unit 1 Desire/Longing
Part one: eager; keen; anxious; desperate; dying to; longing to; feel like   3
Part two: good wishes in letters (formulae); wishing things would change;   6
           wanting to do things; envying other people; imagining things you'd
           like to do

Unit 2 Excitement/Anticipation
Part one: excited about; excited at the thought/prospect of; thrilled; can't wait   12
           to; look forward to
Part two: looking forward to meetings (letter formulae); looking forward to   15
           doing things; sharing other people's excitement; telling people
           exciting news

Unit 3 Worry/Apprehension
Part one: worried; anxious; concerned; nervous; apprehensive; frightened;   20
           terrified; reassure someone/cheer someone up; calm someone down
Part two: worrying about what has happened; worrying about what might   23
           happen; being anxious about other people; not looking forward to
           things; reassuring worried people

Unit 4 Admiration
Part one: impressed; struck; overwhelmed; moved; admire; praise;   29
           compliment; congratulate
Part two: admiring things you see; admiring the way people do things;   33
           complimenting and congratulating people; approving of people's
           actions

Unit 5 Irritation/Impatience
Part one: irritated; annoyed; impatient   38
Part two: getting people to do things; getting people to stop doing things;   41
           waiting for things to happen; getting rid of persistent people

Unit 6 Delight/Relief
Part one: relieved; delighted; pleased; glad; thrilled   46
Part two: greeting and leave-taking (formulae); being glad you've achieved   49
           something; expressing relief after a narrow escape; speculating about

Contents

what might have happened otherwise; showing you are delighted
with something you are given; telling people how much you are
enjoying yourself

Unit 7   Indignation/Annoyance
Part one: annoyed; angry; furious; hurt; offended; indignant; accuse someone   55
of; blame someone for
Part two: expressing anger (formulae); blaming people for what has happened;   58
expressing indignation about other people's actions; being offended
when people let you down

Unit 8   Surprise
Part one: surprised; astonished; amazed; astounded; shocked   65
Part two: expressing surprise when you see something unexpected; reacting   68
with surprise to what you are told; speculating about surprising news

Unit 9   Disappointment/Regret
Part one: tired of; sick of; fed up with; dissatisfied; disappointed; disillusioned;   73
shocked; come as a disappointment/shock to
Part two: apologising in letters; regretting what you have(n't) done; being   76
disappointed with an experience; being disillusioned with your
lifestyle

Unit 10   Interest/Curiosity
Part one: interested; fascinated; intrigued; bored; wonder; be curious to know   83
Part two: making tactful enquiries; speculating about things you see; reacting   86
with interest to what someone tells you

Unit 11   Uncertainty
Part one: puzzled; baffled; confused; can't make out/work out/tell   92
Part two: reacting to a confusing explanation; being uncertain what something   96
is; trying to remember things; being uncertain about what to do

Unit 12   Sympathy and lack of sympathy
Part one: sympathetic; unsympathetic; indifferent; full of sympathy   102
Part two: expressing indifference (formulae); reassuring people; (not) showing   105
sympathy for other people's problems; (not) sympathising with
other people's attitudes

Appendix   Adjectives and verbs used to describe feelings   111

Preface

Feelings arose from the authors' experience in teaching advanced students who felt the need to communicate more effectively in English, and in particular to express their feelings.

The course is intended for upper-intermediate and more advanced students who already have a good grasp of the structures of English, but who need practice in expressing themselves fluently in everyday situations.

Feelings teaches students

a) to *talk about* feelings and situations involving feelings;
b) to *understand* which feelings are being expressed by other people;
c) to *express* feelings in a wide variety of situations.

Each unit provides a variety of stimulating material which encourages students to be imaginative and creative. Many of the activities are for use in pairs and small groups, and include role-play, simulation, discussion, problem-solving and games.

The course is divided into twelve units, each dealing with one broad area of feeling, and provides material for 70–80 classroom hours.

Although not intended as an examination preparation course, *Feelings* is useful for students taking either the Cambridge First Certificate or Proficiency examinations, in the following areas:

a) oral proficiency
b) informal composition
c) vocabulary development

Feelings is accompanied by a Teacher's Book which gives a full account of the linguistic principles on which the course is based, and explains in detail how to teach the material.

Our deepest thanks go to Keith Morrow for his invaluable advice and constructive criticism throughout the development of the course, and also to the many teachers, in particular Janice Abbot, who helped in testing the material.

Adrian Doff
Christopher Jones

Beirut

Acknowledgements

The authors and publishers are grateful to the following for permission to reproduce illustrations:

Punch (pages 6, 15, 33, 41, 49, 59, 68, 86 and 96); Avenue Design Partnership (pages 11 and 35); *Private Eye* (pages 24, 76 and 105); Maggie Stocking (page 28); Camera Press, London (pages 34 and 35); the Trustees of the Victoria and Albert Museum (page 34); Keystone Press Agency (pages 34 and 35); Associated Press (page 35); Barnaby's Picture Library (page 35); Dargaud Editeur (page 42) © Dargaud Editeur Paris 1966 by Goscinny and Uderzo; Scottish Tourist Board (page 81); Peter Baker (page 82); Derek Wood (page 82); Jon Harris (page 88); *Cambridge Evening News* (page 98); Dr Harold Egerton, MIT, Cambridge, Mass. (page 98); Editions Est-Ouest, Brussels (page 100); Gerald Duckworth & Co (page 101).

Drawings by Ted Draper and Martin Salisbury
Book design by Peter Ducker

To the student

Expressing feelings

We express our feelings in some way in almost all the day-to-day language we use. Sometimes we express them very openly and directly (e.g. 'How dare you!' or 'Thank goodness for that!'); at other times, we may be using language for some other purpose, but still our feelings are shown by the expressions we choose and the way we say them (e.g. 'Shut that door, can't you?' or 'I wonder why that letter hasn't come yet').

Because of this, learning to express feelings (and to understand what feelings other people are expressing) is a very important part of learning to use a language.

Talking about feelings

As well as having conversations, we also need to be able to talk *about* conversations we have heard or which we have taken part in ourselves. When we do this, of course, we need to use indirect speech. But we also need to:

a) use particular verbs which express not only what was said, but also how it was said (e.g. 'He *accused* me of lying', 'She *assured* me that everything would be all right').
b) use words that describe people's feelings (e.g. 'He looked very *worried*', 'I found the picture very *intriguing*').
c) use language that describes people's actions (e.g. 'She suddenly burst into tears', 'He stormed out of the room and slammed the door behind him').
d) use language that describes the general scene and the background to the conversation (e.g. 'We were round at Peter's one evening playing cards. . .').

The aim of *feelings*

Feelings teaches both the language we use to express feelings and the language we use to talk about feelings.

Part one of each unit teaches you how to talk *about* situations. It is concerned with all the four kinds of language outlined above, and especially ways of describing people's feelings.

Part two of each unit teaches you how to recognise these feelings, and to express them yourself in a variety of situations.

Each unit will take about six lessons. This is what you will do in a typical unit:

Part one: Talking about the feeling
You will hear a short dialogue which illustrates the feeling covered by the unit, and

learn the language you will need to tell the story of what happens in the dialogue in natural, idiomatic English. Part one is divided into three sections:

A: *Listening and discussion.* You will hear the dialogue and discuss what it is about – who the people are, where they are, how they feel, what happens, and so on.

B: *Practice.* You will learn key expressions for talking about the feeling, and practise them in different situations.

C: *Reporting.* After some final preparation, you will be ready to write a report, telling the story of what happened in the dialogue.

Part two: Expressing the feeling

You will learn how to express the feeling yourself. Part two is divided into three sections:

A: *Recognition.* These exercises, in which you will discuss the implications of various remarks, are designed to give you insight into the language used to express feelings.

B: *Practice.* You will learn key expressions you need to express the feeling in different situations, and practise them in pairs and groups. In these exercises, you will nearly always be *role-playing,* that is, imagining you are someone in a particular situation.

C: *Free expression.* This section consists of much freer activities (both spoken and written), which give you an opportunity to make free use of the language you have learnt.

Unit 1 Desire/Longing

Part one: Talking about the feeling

SECTION A: LISTENING AND DISCUSSION

A1 *Janie: Come on. Everybody else is.*
Peter: Oh Janie! Please!
Janie: Come on! Quick, before it stops.
Peter: But look. You know I. . .
Janie: But it's easy! All you have to do is. . .
Peter: Janie! Why can't we just sit here and talk?
Janie: Huh! I don't know why I came with you in the first place. Now Roger. . .Oh, there he is. Hey, Roger. . .!
Peter: Hey!. . .Janie!

A2 Facts

Discuss these questions.

1 What is the relationship between Janie and Peter?
2 Where are Janie and Peter?
3 What are they doing?
4 What does Janie want to do?
5 Who is Roger?
6 How might Janie's remark 'Now Roger. . .' continue?
7 What does Janie do at the end of the dialogue?

A3 Language

Choose the best answers and justify your choice. More than one answer may be right in each case.

1 Janie . . . . . .
   a) enjoys dancing.
   b) enjoys to dance.
   c) loves dancing.
   d) loves to dance.

3

2 Janie is . . . . . . dancing.
   a) fond on   c) keen on
   b) fond of   d) keen of

3 Janie . . . . . . to dance.
   a) is eager   d) desires
   b) is willing   e) wants
   c) is dying   f) is desperate

4 Janie . . . . . . Peter to dance.
   a) persuades   c) convinces
   b) tries to persuade   d) tries to convince

5 Peter . . . . . .
   a) is reluctant to dance.   d) doesn't like dancing.
   b) doesn't feel like dancing. e) doesn't like to dance.
   c) is unwilling to dance.

6 Peter . . . . . . dance.
   a) won't   c) refuses to
   b) decides not to

SECTION B: PRACTICE

B1 Strength of feeling

Three men apply for the same job.
Mr A is *eager* (or *keen*) *to* get the job. He thinks the job will suit him and that he'll enjoy the work very much.
Mr B is *anxious to* get the job. He's getting married soon and wants a secure future.
Mr C is *desperate to* get the job. He has already tried to get lots of other jobs, but nobody will employ him.

What do each of the people below want to do? Talk about each one, using the most appropriate expression from the list in each case.

eager to
keen to
anxious to
desperate to

Example
John: 'There's a great film on at the Odeon. Do let's go and see it.'
Answer: John was very keen to see the film.

  1 Lawrence: 'If I don't find water soon, I'll die.'
  2 George: 'I really ought to get married soon. After all, I'm over 35 already.'
  3 Anna: 'Can I show you my stamp collection? I'm sure you'd like it.'

4 Carol: 'Yes, I'd love to go riding. I've never tried it before.'

5 James: 'For God's sake get a doctor. My wife's just collapsed.'

6 Alan: 'Do you know a good dentist? One of my fillings seems to be giving me a bit of trouble.'

▶ How could Janie and Peter use this language to talk about what happened?

B2 Story line

Look at the examples, and then make similar reports from the notes below. Use the expressions in italics in your answers.

Example 1

We were sitting at home the other evening, and Alex was watching TV as usual. I $\left|\begin{matrix} was\ dying \\ was\ longing \end{matrix}\right|$ to go out for a change. But when I suggested it, he *didn't seem* at all $\left|\begin{matrix} keen\ on\ the\ idea. \\ interested. \end{matrix}\right|$ *All he wanted to do was* sit there in front of the TV.

Example 2

We were watching 'Sportsnight' the other night, when Irene suddenly *decided* she *wanted* to go out. I $\left|\begin{matrix} wasn't\ in\ the\ mood\ to\ go \\ didn't\ feel\ like\ going \end{matrix}\right|$ anywhere. I was quite $\left|\begin{matrix} happy\ to \\ content\ to \end{matrix}\right|$ watch TV.

1 Driving in the country/Stop and go for a walk.

2 Sitting in the pub/Go and visit Charlie and Mavis.

3 Playing draughts/Teach him or her how to play chess.

Now think up a situation of your own and make a report.

▶ How could Janie and Peter use this language to talk about what happened?

SECTION C: REPORTING

C1 Imagine that either Janie or Peter is telling a friend about what happened. How might they use the following expressions?

to be crazy about
to fancy
to do one's best to
to talk someone out of something
embarrassed
jealous
excuse

C2 Now imagine that you are either a) Janie or b) Peter, telling a friend about what happened. Write a report, using the language you have practised where you think it is appropriate.

Part two: Expressing the feeling

SECTION A: RECOGNITION

 A1 Who wants what?

All the remarks below are replies to what someone has just said. Suggest situations in which they might be said, and what they might be replies to.

1 I wouldn't be averse to a drop myself.
   Example answer: Two people both want a drink. It could be a reply to 'I think I'll have a brandy'. The speaker is saying he wants one too.
2 Mm. A bit of sun would make all the difference, wouldn't it?
3 Awful. In fact, if it weren't for the kids, we'd move tomorrow.
4 Love one. I haven't had a thing all day.
5 I hope it does. That'll teach them to keep going on strike.
6 I only wish I could. I just haven't got the will-power, that's the trouble.
7 With a house thrown in? Now you're talking!
8 Speech!

'I don't want your money – I want your easygoing charm, your wealth of knowledge, your talent to amuse...'

A2 Best wishes

Look at the following extracts from letters, all of which express good wishes.

Best wishes for a speedy recovery.
I wish you the very best of luck.
Wishing you good health and lots of happiness.
May I wish you every success for the future.
Hope you have a great time.
Hoping you'll be up and about again soon.
I hope you have a pleasant and enjoyable stay.
Keeping my fingers crossed for you.

1 Which two extracts would you expect to find in letters to:
   a) someone who's retiring
   b) someone who's got the 'flu
   c) someone who's going on holiday
   d) someone who's giving his first solo performance in a concert

2 In each case, say which of the two extracts you would expect to be followed by 'Yours sincerely, Gerald Fox', and which by 'Love, Gerry'.

SECTION B: PRACTICE

B1 Wishful thinking

1 In each of the pictures below, the people are hoping that things will change, but don't think it very likely.

What other changes might they be hoping for? What might they say? Use these expressions where appropriate:

I wish. . .would. . .   I wish I/we could. . .
If only. . .would. . .   If only I/we could. . .

7

2 Now decide what the pavement artist in the picture is wishing would happen. Make captions similar to those above.

3 Work in pairs.

Student A: Imagine you are in one of the situations below. Make remarks using 'I wish. . .', or, 'If only. . .'

Student B: Reply in any appropriate way.

Examples

A: I wish it would rain.

B: Yes, it's getting terribly dry, isn't it?

A: If only the sun would come out.

B: Yes, that would be nice, wouldn't it?

a) The weather is bad.
b) You're trying to sell your house.
c) You're on a desert island.
d) You're hitchhiking on an empty road.
e) You've read that inflation is getting worse.

B2 Mild and strong

Humphrey expresses his desires quite
mildly. Godfrey, on the other hand,
expresses his desires very strongly. For
example, Humphrey might say 'I'd quite
like a drink', whereas Godfrey would say
'I'd love a drink'.
Here are some other ways they might
express their desire for a drink:

I wouldn't mind a drink.
It'd be nice to have a drink.
I'm dying for a drink.
I feel like a drink.
I've just got to have a drink.
I rather fancy a drink.
I'd give anything for a drink.

1   Which remarks are more likely to be made by Humphrey, and which by Godfrey?
    And how would they be said?

2   What could a) Humphrey and b) Godfrey say about:
    a swim   a pair of binoculars
    going for a swim   seeing a film

3   Work in pairs.
    Look at the picture, and improvise conversations like the one below.
    Use all the expressions in your answers.

    Godfrey: I'd give anything to have a go on that helter-skelter.
    Humphrey: Yes, I wouldn't mind a ride on it myself.

B3   A vicious circle

Each of the people in the pictures is envious of the person in the picture next to him, and wishes he were like him.

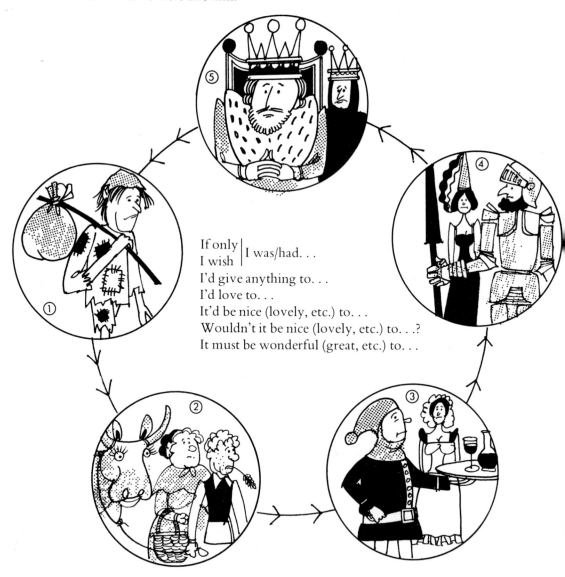

If only | I was/had. . .
I wish |
I'd give anything to. . .
I'd love to. . .
It'd be nice (lovely, etc.) to. . .
Wouldn't it be nice (lovely, etc.) to. . .?
It must be wonderful (great, etc.) to. . .

1 Who do you think each person is? What does he envy about the next person?
2 What do you think each person might be saying or thinking? Use the expressions listed above where appropriate.
3 Join your ideas together to tell the story that the pictures represent.

SECTION C: FREE EXPRESSION

C1 Merry-go-round

THE SOCIAL CLUB FOR VISITORS TO LONDON

FED UP with museums?
BORED with feeding pigeons in Trafalgar Square?
Let us show you what ELSE you can do in London.
We know all the things to do, all the places
to go — and lots of other people like you.
Here's all you do:
Simply write us a letter. Tell us the things you'd
really like to do in London. And that means *anything*:

PEOPLE   **HOBBIES AND INTERESTS**
ENTERTAINMENT   **EVENING CLASSES**
PRIVATE PARTIES **EVEN MUSEUMS IF YOU WANT!**

Then just sit back and wait for your
first invitation!

Write to:
Merry Go Round, 3A, Grimsby Terrace,   Enclose cheque
Watford, Herts.   for £50

C2 Just the job

'. . .Oh, I think it'd be a great job. You'd really be sure you were doing people some good. Of course, they might not seem to like you very much, but you'd know they appreciated you really. And think of the power – that's what I'd like about it. You could stand there talking about whatever you liked, and they wouldn't even be able to open their mouths – or rather, close them. . .'

1 What job do you think the speaker is talking about?
2 Choose a job that you'd like to have (not necessarily one which you expect to have yourself).
   Imagine that you are talking to a friend about the job. Without actually naming the job, explain to him why you would like it. Give enough clues (but not too many) so that it is possible to guess what job it is.

Unit 2 Excitement/Anticipation

Part one: Talking about the feeling

SECTION A: LISTENING AND DISCUSSION

 A1 *John: ...Come on, Gladstone! Come on!*

Bill: You know, John...he could just make it.

John: Come on! You can do it!

Bill: If he can only get past Evening Glow...

John: He's up there – he's going to do it...Yes!...

Bill: He's there! We've done it!

John: Two hundred to one! Just wait till I get down to that bookie!

Bill: Phew! Just think of all the things we'll be able to...

John: We? It was me that placed the bet, you know...

A2 Facts

Discuss these questions.

1 What is the relationship between John and Bill?
2 Explain 'Gladstone' and 'Evening Glow'.
3 Where are John and Bill and what are they doing?
4 What is happening when Bill says 'He's there!'?
5 Where is John going to go, and why?
6 How might Bill's sentence 'Just think of all the things we'll be able to...' continue?
7 What is the point of John's last remark?

A3 Language

Choose the best answers and justify your choices. More than one answer may be right in each case.

1 John and Bill find the race ......
   a) very exciting.   c) absolutely exciting.
   b) very excited.   d) absolutely excited.

2 As the race goes on, they get more and more . . . . . .
   a) exciting.   c) excitable.
   b) excited.

3 They are . . . . . . with the result.
   a) delighted   c) thrilled
   b) delightful   d) thrilling

4 John is . . . . . . that Gladstone is going to win.
   a) confident   d) sure
   b) self-confident e) certain
   c) assured

5 They . . . . . . to go to the bookie.
   a) are expecting   c) can't wait
   b) are waiting

6 They are looking forward . . . . . . their winnings.
   a) for spend   c) to spend
   b) for spending   d) to spending

7 They feel excited . . . . . . spending the money.
   a) about   c) at the prospect of
   b) at the thought of

SECTION B: PRACTICE

B1 Exciting prospects

Philip has just won a competition; the first prize is a free holiday in Rome. He's
leaving next week. While he's there, he plans to eat pizza at least twice a day. He also
intends to visit the Coliseum.

He's *excited about* winning the competition.
He's *excited about* going to Rome.

He's *excited at the* | *prospect* / *thought* | *of* eating so many pizzas.

He's *excited at the* | *prospect* / *thought* | *of* visiting the Coliseum.

13

1 What is the difference between *excited about,* and *excited at the thought/prospect of?*
2 What are these people excited about? What might they be excited at the thought/prospect of doing?

a) Edward has just become Director of the National Theatre.
b) Jack is a zoologist. He's going on an expedition to Borneo.
c) Carolyn is leaving the village she grew up in and going to live in London.
d) Susie Swingle, aged 16, has just become a pop star.
e) Ron has just been accepted by Cambridge University.

▶ How could Bill use this language to talk about what happened?

B2 Story line

Look at the example and tell similar stories based on the titles and notes below. Use the expressions in italics in your answers.

Example
Title: HOW I BECAME THE FIRST WOMAN ON THE MOON (degree in astrophysics – interview)
Story: 'Well, when I heard that they wanted a woman with a degree in astrophysics, I knew that I $\left|\begin{matrix} stood \\ had \end{matrix}\right|$ *a good chance of* getting the job. $\left|\begin{matrix} But\ it\ was\ only\ when \\ But\ it\ wasn't\ until \end{matrix}\right|$ they invited me for an interview *that I really started getting excited.* Two weeks later I got the job. I was $\left|\begin{matrix} thrilled\ to\ bits. \\ absolutely\ thrilled. \end{matrix}\right|$ I $\left|\begin{matrix} couldn't\ wait\ to \\ could\ hardly\ wait\ to \end{matrix}\right|$ get my spacesuit on. . .'

1 HOW I BECAME MISS WORLD (long legs and red hair – the final)
2 HOW I GOT STAR ROLE IN ROCK OPERA '*HAMLET*' (singer with acting experience – audition)
3 HOW OUR RECORD BECAME A NUMBER ONE HIT (good review – played on 'Top of the Pops')

▶ How could Bill use this language to talk about what happened?

SECTION C: REPORTING

C1 John decided to share his money with Bill after all. They set up a business together, and later became multi-millionaires. Bill is writing an article entitled 'How I became a millionaire'. How might he use the following expressions in his article?

to bet on	to collect
odds	to keep for oneself
to catch up with	turning point

C2 Now imagine that you are Bill, writing the article. Write the part of the article where he talks about the horse-race.

Part two: Expressing the feeling

SECTION A: RECOGNITION

A1 Breathless moments

Look at the remarks below. Decide who the people are, what they're doing, and what they're excited about.

1 Ssh – look! A golden eagle! See the shape of the wings?
2 Come on, United! After 'em!
3 Yes, go on! Take his bishop! *That's* right!
4 Over there – on the horizon! Quick, get a fire going!
5 Ladies and Gentlemen. This is indeed a proud moment for me and, I trust, for all my supporters who turned out in such large numbers today. . .
6 See? 5.23 centimetres. Much too big for an ape.
7 Wait a minute. . .I know. It's. . .No, don't tell me. . .

It's Spring, Arthur, Spring!

A2 Postbag

Look at the following extracts from letters, in which the writers are looking forward to a meeting.

1 . . .I'm counting the days till the 17th. . .
2 . . .looking forward to seeing you on the 17th. . .
3 . . .see you on the 17th. . .
4 . . .I look forward to our meeting on 17 February. . .
5 . . .it'll be really great to actually meet you at last. . .
6 . . .it'll be good to get together again. . .

Which extract would you expect to see in a letter from:

a) a businessman you've never met
b) a businessman you often do business with
c) a penfriend
d) a close friend
e) an old friend who you haven't seen for a long time
f) someone who's in love with you

Which extracts express excitement most openly? Mark them on the scale below:

LEAST EXCITED: | | | | | | | :MOST EXCITED

SECTION B: PRACTICE

B1 Changes of scene

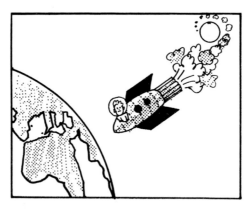

Look at this picture of a spaceship returning to Earth. Here are some of the things the people in the spaceship might be saying:

I'm really looking forward to being back on Earth.
I can't wait to get out of this spacesuit!
Won't it be nice to be able to lie in the sun again!
Just think of all that green grass!
The first thing I'm going to do when I get back is go for a swim.

1 Look at the pictures below. Who are the people in them, and what do you think they're looking forward to?
Make captions for the pictures, similar to those above. Use the topics listed underneath to help you.

food	food	entertainment
rest	money	people
people	people	shopping
movement	interests	movement

2 Work in pairs.
Imagine you are in these situations, and improvise a conversation.

   a) Two bank clerks are about to retire. They are both keen gardeners.
   b) Two people are coming back from a camping holiday in the rain.
   c) Two caterpillars are looking forward to becoming butterflies.

B2 Lucky you!

1 Here are some ways in which April's friends show their excitement when they hear her good news. Complete their remarks.
2 How might April reply to each remark?

3 Work in groups.
Each member of the group tells the others a piece of good news about himself/herself. This can be real or imaginary. The others react appropriately, and show their excitement by using some of the expressions above. Each time, continue as long as you can.
Here are some ideas:

   a) You're going to visit an interesting place.
   b) You've just bought or been given something.
   c) You've been invited to a party.
   d) You're going to meet somebody famous.
   e) Somebody you haven't seen for a long time is coming to visit you.

B3   Have you heard?

NEW BRITISH SUPERSONIC AIRLINER BUILT
Flying time to New York will be halved

Jack: Hey! Have you heard the news? . . . . . .

Jill: Yes, I read about it.
| It didn't seem . . . . . .
| I didn't think . . . . . .
| It didn't strike me as . . . . . .

Jack: But just | imagine! | People will be able to . . . . . .
                 | think of it! |

Jill: Yes, but . . . . . . already . . . . . .

Jack: But | don't you realise? | It'll mean that . . . . . .
            | don't you see? |

Jill: Hmm, yes. I suppose . . . : . . .

Jack: | Exactly! | And | what's more, | . . . . . .
        | Precisely! | | not only that, |

Jill: Hmm, yes. You could be right. Maybe . . . . . .

1 a) Why do you think Jack is excited about the new airliner? Complete his
       remarks.
   b) Complete Jill's remarks.
   c) In pairs, act out the conversation.

2 Work in pairs.
   a) Look at the newspaper headlines below. What are they about?
   b) In each case, think of some reasons why Jack is excited about the news.
   c) Imagine that you are Jack and Jill. Improvise similar conversations, based on the
       newspaper headlines.

       CHANNEL TUNNEL BEING BUILT
       Direct road link to France by next year

       VIDEO TELEPHONES NOW AVAILABLE IN BRITAIN
       'Sight and Sound' calls now possible

       'DEMOCRATIC' LOCAL TV STATIONS PLANNED
       Viewers to make their own programmes

SECTION C: FREE EXPRESSION

C1 **Old and new**

Holiday Camp to be built at Brinscombe

unemployment to Brinscombe, and the camp will provide more than 500 jobs. Amenities will include a five-star hotel, with nightclub and discotheque. The camp will have its own cinema, a heated swimming pool and possibly a casino.

It has been decided to build a holiday camp just outside the tiny fishing village of Brinscombe, in Devon. The decline of the fishing industry has brought a lot of

---

Work in pairs.

Pair A: You are Freda. You are 22, single, unemployed and bored. When you read about the holiday camp, you are very excited.

You see Mrs Mullet in the pub. She is 60 years old and very conservative, and you can guess that she is horrified by the news. You want to tell her how excited you are, and to convince her that the holiday camp is a good thing. Decide what you are excited about and why. Work out what you will say to Mrs Mullet.

Pair B: You are Mrs Mullet. You are 60, from a traditional fishing family, and you don't want Brinscombe to change. When you read about the holiday camp, you are horrified.

You see Freda in the pub. She is 22 and very modern, and you can guess that she is excited about the news.

Decide why you don't like the idea of the holiday camp. Work out what you will say to Freda.

Now form new pairs (A and B together this time) and improvise the conversation.

C2 **What's new?**

Here is part of a letter. The writer is excited about something he has just invented. From the information in the letter, guess what the invention is.

DEAR X
I'VE JUST INVENTED SOMETHING QUITE AMAZING : A
COMPLETELY NEW METHOD OF MOVING THINGS. I KNOW
YOU WON'T BELIEVE ME, BUT WITH THIS INVENTION
A SINGLE HORSE COULD PULL TEN TIMES ITS OWN
WEIGHT! IT COULD COMPLETELY REVOLUTIONIZE OUR
TRANSPORT SYSTEM! I SIMPLY CAN'T WAIT TO SHOW
IT TO YOU. IT'S SO BEAUTIFULLY SIMPLE. THE IDEA
CAME TO ME THE OTHER DAY WHEN I WAS CHOPPING
UP A TREE . . .

Think of another invention which is now a common object (anything from matches to a jet plane). Write part of an excited letter from the inventor to a friend/colleague telling him about the invention. Give enough clues (but not too many) so that it is possible to guess what the invention is.

Unit 3 Worry/Apprehension

Part one: Talking about the feeling

SECTION A: LISTENING AND DISCUSSION

A1 *Mrs Ponsonby:* *. . .but it's been three days now. What on earth could have happened to him? I mean, I can't believe he would have gone off just like that. It's so unlike him. . .Oh, dear, I do hope he's all right. . .It's all my fault. I should never have. . .*

Mr Steadman: *Now don't you worry, Mrs Ponsonby. We'll find him. After all, he can't have gone far. Now then. Answers to the name of Augustus, you said. . .*

A2 Facts

Discuss these questions.

1 Who is Mr Steadman?
2 Where does the conversation take place?
3 Who is Augustus?
4 What happened three days ago?
5 How might Mrs Ponsonby's remark 'I should never have. . .' continue?
6 What is Mr Steadman doing when he says 'Now then'?

A3 Language

Choose the best answers and justify your choices. More than one answer may be right in each case.

1 Mrs Ponsonby is . . . . . . about Augustus.
  a) worried   d) frightened
  b) nervous   e) anxious
  c) apprehensive

2 Mr Steadman is, or pretends to be, concerned . . . . . . Mrs Ponsonby's problem.
  a) about   c) in
  b) with

3 Mrs Ponsonby is . . . . . . with worry.
   a) wild   c) out of her mind
   b) frantic

4 Mr Steadman tries to . . . . . . Mrs Ponsonby.
   a) insure   c) reassure
   b) assure

5 Mr Steadman . . . . . . Mrs Ponsonby that Augustus will be found.
   a) insures   c) reassures
   b) assures

SECTION B: PRACTICE

B1 Strength of feeling

Mary was going to fly to New York. She had never flown before, so she felt a bit *nervous*. After they took off, the captain announced that they were expecting very bad weather. This made her *apprehensive*. As they flew into the storm clouds, she began to get *frightened*. Then suddenly there was a flash of lightning, and the plane dropped 30 feet. Mary was absolutely *terrified*. . .

1 What is the difference between *nervous, apprehensive, frightened* and *terrified*?
2 Now use one of these words to say how you would feel in each of the following situations:
   a) You are going for an interview for a job.
   b) You are not doing very well in your new job. Your boss has just asked you to come into his office.
   c) You're starting a new job tomorrow.
   d) You're walking through a graveyard at night, and one of the gravestones begins to move.
   e) Your Great Aunt Bertha, who you can't stand, is coming to stay with you for a month.

B2 Shades of meaning

Worried, anxious and *concerned* mean almost the same thing, and can often be used as alternatives.

e.g. Mrs Tomkins isn't at all well. We're all very | worried / anxious / concerned | about her.

Anxious is used especially when you're afraid that something *might* | happen. / have happened.

e.g. Mr Blythe doesn't think that his new play has been rehearsed enough, and the first performance is tomorrow. He's very *worried/anxious* about it.

Concerned is used especially when you're worried about *someone else's* problems.
e.g. John's not doing very well at school. His teachers are *worried/concerned* about him.

Mr Green, a factory worker, is about to have a serious operation. After the operation, he'll have to rest for six months before going back to work.
Use the notes below to talk about the feelings of a) Mr Green, b) Mrs Green, c) his doctor, d) his workmates.

worried   go back/work
anxious   success/operation
concerned   lose/job
                   health

B3 Story line

Look at the example and make similar reports from the remarks below, one for each person involved. Use the expressions in italics in your answers.

Example
Mrs Brown: It'll be all right, dear – I'm sure he'll get over it soon. Let's have a nice cup of tea.

Later
Mrs Green: I was | *out of my mind* / *frantic* | with worry about poor George's operation. But

Mrs Brown *really* | *cheered me up* / *made me feel a lot better* | and made me a nice cup of tea.

Mrs Brown: Poor Mrs Green, she was so worried about George. She

| *wouldn't stop talking* / *kept on and on* | about him. I tried to | *reassure* her. / *put* her *mind at rest.* | We had a

nice cup of tea together and she felt much better.

  1 Dr James to Mr Matthews:
     'Oh, it's nothing to worry about. It's perfectly natural at your age. Now if you're

22

still worried about it, come and see me again next week. Meanwhile, take two of these three times a day. . .'

2 Mr Fraser to Mrs Nelson:
'He'll be all right. Why, at his age, I was always risking my neck, and I loved every minute of it. Look at this – that's me, right at the top. Only 16, I was, and my mother would've gone crazy if she'd known. . .'

3 Jim to Anthony:
'Nonsense. I'm sure there are lots of jobs for people with a degree in Latin. There's the Civil Service, teaching. . .um. . .Anyway, there's no point in worrying about it. Let's go and have a drink.'

▶ How could Mrs Ponsonby and Mr Steadman use this language to talk about what happened?

SECTION C: REPORTING

C1 Imagine that either Mrs Ponsonby or Mr Steadman is telling a friend about what happened. How might they use the following expressions?

upset	patiently
afraid	to calm down
to blame	to take down
guilty	

C2 Now imagine you are either a) Mrs Ponsonby or b) Mr Steadman telling a friend about what happened. Write a report, using the language you have practised where you think it is appropriate.

Part two: Expressing the feeling

SECTION A: RECOGNITION

A1 A bundle of nerves

Look at the remarks below. Decide who the people are, what they're doing and why they're worried.

1 I suppose they *are* only cows, aren't they?
2 Seven already? Oh well. Here goes.
3 . . .Yes, this is Mrs Hansford – but how do you know my name? Who are you?
4 Nonsense. It's only a mouse – at least. . .
5 Mm. Sharper than they look, these bends, aren't they?

6 What? The last one? Oh no. I'll never last out till morning.

7 So that's 115 and 35, plus another 60 for the party – that makes. . .oh dear.

"She's afraid they might re-open the line without telling us."

A2 Lost in the post

George is expecting an extremely important letter to arrive on September 1st. When it doesn't arrive by September 5th, he begins to get a little worried; by the end of the month he is desperate. Here are some things that he says on different days in September, after the postman has been, and some things his room-mate says to reassure him. Match the dates with the remarks and replies.

A	If that letter doesn't come soon, I don't know what I'll do	Sept. 5th	It'll come, don't worry.
B	It really ought to have come by now.	Sept. 10th	Now try not to get too upset about it. We'll all do what we can to help.
C	It must come, It must. I just can't think what I'll do without it.	Sept. 15th	I don't expect they've got round to replying yet.
D	I wonder why it hasn't come yet.	Sept. 20th	Oh, I'm sure it'll turn up soon. You know what the post is like these days.
E	It ought to have got here days ago. Whatever can have happened?	Sept. 25th	Try not to worry. There's bound to be some simple explanation.

SECTION B: PRACTICE

B1 Alarming thoughts

The woman in the picture is worried about her handbag. Here are some of the things she might be saying:

I hope it turns up somewhere.
Supposing it's been stolen.
Oh dear. I wonder if I left it on the train.
If I don't find it, *I don't know* what I'll do.
If only I could remember where I put it.
What if somebody finds it and doesn't give it back?

1 Look at the pictures below. What has happened to the people in them, and what kinds of things do you think they're worried about?
Make captions for these pictures, similar to those above.

2 Work in pairs or groups.
Imagine you are in these situations, and that you are worried. Together, discuss your problem. Use any of the expressions above where you think they are appropriate.

    a) You are meeting someone in London to discuss some important business. The man still hasn't turned up, and he's an hour late.
    b) You have eaten some sea-food in a restaurant. You all feel rather ill.
    c) You are robbing a safe when you hear footsteps coming towards the house.
    d) You are sitting in a restaurant when you hear a loud explosion nearby.

B2   Far from home

Peter's mother is very worried about him. This is what she says to her husband:

'Oh dear. *I do hope* Peter's all right. . .But *supposing* he's got lost. . .Yes, but he *might've* broken his ankle. . .But *what if* he runs out of food?. . .And *what about* all those wild animals? He *could've* been attacked by a bear, or something. . .Well, if he's all right, why hasn't he telephoned?'

1 a) Peter's father is not at all worried.
       What replies do you think he might make?
   b) In pairs, act out the conversation between Peter's mother and father.

2 Work in pairs.
   Improvise similar conversations about the following, using the expressions in list.
   I do hope. . .   Supposing. . .
   What about. . .   . . .could. . .
   . . .might. . .   What if. . .

   a) Your 20-year-old son Robert is crossing the Sahara on a motor-bike.
   b) Your 18-year-old daughter Anne has gone sailing.
   c) Your 16-year-old son Richard has gone hitch-hiking abroad.

B3   Cold feet

Malcolm has just completed his training as a teacher. He's feeling very apprehensive. He is talking to Janet at a party.

Janet:	I expect you're quite looking forward to teaching, aren't you?	
Malcolm:	Well, actually	I'm (absolutely) dreading it.
	To tell you the truth	I'm not looking forward to it at all.
	As a matter of fact	I'm rather worried about it.
Janet:	Oh, really? How's that, then?	
Malcolm:	I just don't think I'll be able to. . .	
	Oh, it's just the thought of. . .	
Janet:	Oh, I see.	
Malcolm:	You see, the trouble is. . .	
	And it's not only that. It's. . .	

1 a) Think of some reasons why Malcolm might be apprehensive, and complete his remarks.

   b) In pairs, act out the conversation, continuing in any way you like. Janet may agree or disagree with what Malcolm says.

2 Work in pairs.
   Choose four of these situations, and improvise similar conversations.

   a) You are about to become a TV announcer.
   b) You are about to retire.
   c) You are going to work as a tourist guide for the summer.
   d) You are going to give a solo performance in a concert next week.
   e) You have been invited to a party at the British Embassy.
   f) You are getting married next month.
   g) You are about to become King.

SECTION C: FREE EXPRESSION

C1 Psychiatrist's couch

A psychiatrist is about to interview a new patient. He has already spoken to the boy's parents. Here are the notes which he took during his interview with them:

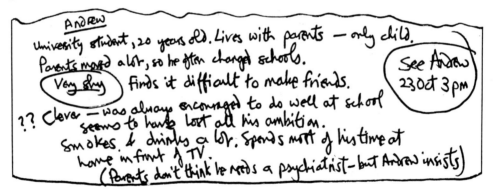

Work in pairs.
Pair A: You are Andrew. You're very worried about your situation, and are sure that the psychiatrist can help you. You know he has already spoken to your parents, and you are afraid that he may not take your problems very seriously.
        The psychiatrist will want to know all about your problems. Work out what questions he might ask, and what you will tell him.
Pair B: You are the psychiatrist. You're not sure how serious Andrew's problems are, and you want to find out much more about them.
        Work out what questions you will ask him (remembering that he is very shy), and how you might reassure him.

Now form new pairs and improvise the interview.

C2 What's up?

1 Choose one of the six photographs below, each of which shows a worried person. Decide who and where the person is, what his/her problems are and what he/she is worried about. The problems should in some way be related to the photograph.
2 Write a letter from the person to a friend (or a magazine), expressing his/her worry. Give enough clues (but not too many) so that it is possible to guess which photograph you have chosen.

Unit 4 Admiration

Part one: Talking about the feeling

SECTION A: LISTENING AND DISCUSSION

A1 *Clarence:* *Ooh, I say – now that's lovely! Where did you get it?*
George: *That? Oh, that's just an old vase I found in the attic. Why, do you like it?*
Clarence: *Oh, I think it's marvellous! It's – it's so elegant somehow – so dignified!*
George: *Well, if you really like it, you can have it.*
Clarence: *Oh, but I'd love to have it. I really would! But you're quite sure you don't want it yourselves?*
George: *Well, to be honest, we'd be quite glad to have it taken off our hands*

A2 Facts

Discuss these questions.

1 What do you think is the relationship between Clarence and George?
2 Where do you think they are?
3 What is Clarence doing during the conversation?
4 What do the words 'elegant' and 'dignified' tell you about the vase?
5 What do you think George thinks of the vase?
6 What do you think George thinks of Clarence?
7 What do you think Clarence thinks of George?

A3 Language

Choose the best answers and justify your choices. More than one answer may be right in each case.
1 Clarence is . . . . . .by the vase.
   a) impressed
   b) moved
   c) struck
   d) overwhelmed

29

2 Clarence . . . . . . the vase.
  a) praises
  b) is full of praise for
  c) admires
  d) is full of admiration for
  e) compliments
  f) congratulates

3 He is . . . . . . to have the vase.
  a) willing
  b) keen
  c) eager
  d) anxious
  e) desperate

4 George doesn't . . . . . . the vase.
  a) approve of
  b) think much of
  c) estimate

5 He is glad to . . . . . . it.
  a) free himself from
  b) get free from
  c) rid himself of
  d) get rid of

6 George offers . . . . . .
  a) Clarence to have it.
  b) to let Clarence have it.
  c) Clarence the vase.
  d) to give it to Clarence.
  e) Clarence to give it to him.

7 Clarence is, or pretends to be, ... of antiques.
  a) a lover
  b) an amateur
  c) a connoisseur

SECTION B: PRACTICE

B1 First impressions

Françoise went to Athens for the first time. The first night she had dinner in an open-air restaurant at the foot of the Acropolis.

She was *most impressed* by the service.
She found the service *most impressive*.

She was *quite struck* by the waiters' costumes.
She found the waiters' costumes *quite striking*.

She was *quite overwhelmed* by the sight of the Acropolis.
She found the sight of the Acropolis *quite overwhelming*.

She was *very moved* by the beautiful Greek music.
She found the beautiful Greek music *very moving*.

1 What is the difference between *impressed, struck, overwhelmed* and *moved*?

2 Here are some things that Françoise wrote on her postcards home during the rest of her holiday. Say how she felt, choosing appropriate expressions from the list above.

a) The ferry services are excellent.
b) The views from the boat are magnificent.
c) A lot of the men have great big curly moustaches.
d) The sunset this evening brought tears to my eyes.
e) The people here are incredibly friendly.
f) I've never seen houses with such dazzling white walls before.
g) Went to see a Greek tragedy last night – in the open air! What an experience!

B2 Words of praise

To admire: You can admire
a) things you are actually looking at.
    e.g. He sat there *admiring* the view.
        He *admired* my latest painting.
        (=He gazed at it and said, or thought to himself, how beautiful it was.)
b) People's characters, abilities and achievements.
    e.g. John *admired* his grandmother.
        John *admired* his grandmother's paintings.
        (=He thought she was a wonderful person and a good artist – but he didn't necessarily tell anyone.)

To praise: You can praise people and their achievements.
e.g. 'You've painted that very well.   He *praised* my painting.
    'Leeds have never shown so much   The newspaper *praised* Leeds *for*
    skill as they did yesterday.'   the skill they had shown in the
                                    match.

To compliment: You can compliment people.
e.g. 'You're looking wonderful.'   He *complimented* her *on* her appearance.

To congratulate: You can congratulate people.
e.g. 'Well run, Jim.'   Jim's friends *congratulated* him *on* winning the race.

You got a new job recently, and you gave a party to celebrate. It was very successful, and your guests were very polite. Here are some of the things that happened:

1 As they arrived, they all shook you warmly by the hand.
2 You/Your wife had a new dress on.
3 You cooked a perfect dinner.
4 You showed them round the garden.
5 Your daughter recited a piece on the piano.
6 You served your best vintage wine.
7 Your son showed them the model aeroplanes he had built.

Talk about how your guests reacted to these things. Use the expressions in the list:

to admire	full of admiration	to compliment
to praise	full of praise	to congratulate

▶ How could Clarence and George use this language to talk about what happened?

SECTION C: REPORTING

C1 Imagine that Clarence or George is telling a friend about what happened. How might they use the following expressions?

to notice	to accept
to my surprise	delighted
value	to appreciate

C2 Now imagine that you are either a) Clarence or b) George, writing to a friend about what happened.
Write the part of the letter that describes the incident, using the language you have practised where you think it is appropriate.

Part two: Expressing the feeling

SECTION A: RECOGNITION

A1 Good for you

Look at the following remarks, and suggest situations in which they are appropriate.

1 You were wonderful. We were all so proud of you.
2 It's lovely. It must have taken you hours.
3 I don't know how you manage to put up with them all day long.
4 I've always admired your work very much.
5 To the best Mum in all the world.
6 You seem to be coming along very well.
7 Accurate and well expressed. You have interesting ideas.
8 You *are* a sweet little thing, aren't you? Yes you are, aren't you?

'Oh, darling! It's just like the brochure.'

A2 Put in a good word

Look at the remarks below. In each one, replace the word 'fantastic' with one of the words in the list that follows, to make the meaning more precise.

1 Mm. This chocolate's fantastic.
2 Saw Chitty-Chitty Bang-Bang last night. It's a fantastic film.
3 Mr Springle's fantastic, isn't he? I knew you'd like him.
4 You really must come parachuting some time – it's a fantastic experience.
5 I think I'll see Mr Sly – they say he's a fantastic lawyer.
6 Nobody ever comes down here. It'd be a fantastic place to commit a murder. . .

brilliant	charming
ideal	unforgettable
delightful	delicious

In the remarks above, 'fantastic' means 'very good indeed'. Think of some other English words that are used like 'fantastic'.

SECTION B: PRACTICE

B1 Introvert Irene and extrovert Ernie

Irene and Ernie are twins. They both like the same things, but Ernie expresses his feelings much more strongly than Irene. In the picture, they are admiring a piece of sculpture. Here are some of the things they might be saying:

Irene	*Ernie*
Oh look. That one's not bad.	Just look at that sculpture! Isn't it amazing!
I think that's quite pretty. Don't you?	I've never seen such a beautiful piece of sculpture!
That's rather a clever idea, isn't it?	What a brilliant idea!
Mm. I like that. It's nice and simple.	Now that's absolutely superb! It's so fantastically simple!
It seems sort of. . .optimistic, somehow.	I *do* think that's clever! The way it sums up the human condition so magnificently. . .

Work in pairs.
One of you is Irene, the other is Ernie. Together, admire the things in the photographs.

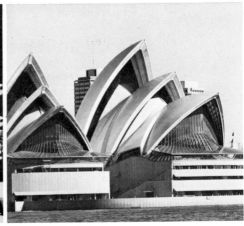

B2 How do you do it?

1 a) What do you think Mrs Brown can do better, now that she takes ENERGEX?
   b) What do you think everyone is saying to her?
   c) What modest replies do you think she might make?

2 Work in groups.
   Admire each other in a similar way, using the expressions above.
   When it's your turn to be admired, make suitably modest replies.
   Either say real things about the person being admired, or make some up. Here are
   some ideas:

   style of dress
   English
   hard work
   sport
   character

B3 Cheering news

Cigarettes to go up 50%

Jones: Good Lord! They're putting cigarettes up by 50%!

Smith: | Good for them!
| Quite right too!
| Are they? Good.
| A good thing too.

Jones: Oh! Why do you say that?

Smith: | I think they're quite right to . . . . . .
| I think it's an excellent idea to . . . . . .
| I thoroughly approve of . . .ing . . . . . .

Jones: | But they could've . . .
| But there was no need to . . . . . .

1 a) Complete Smith's second remark.
   b) Complete Jones's reply.
   c) How might the conversation continue?
   d) In pairs, act out the conversation between Jones and Smith, continuing for as long as you can.

2 Work in pairs.
   a) Look at the newspaper headlines below. What are they about?
   b) Imagine that you are Smith and Jones. Improvise similar conversations, based on the newspaper headlines.

   DOGS BANNED FROM SHOPPING AREA

   CAR PARK PROTEST: 'WE NEED CHILDREN'S PLAYGROUND' SAY ANGRY RESIDENTS

   SECRETARY SACKED FOR REFUSING TO MAKE COFFEE

   MAN FINED £50 FOR DROPPING LITTER

   SCHOOL LEAVING AGE TO BE LOWERED TO 14

SECTION C: FREE EXPRESSION

C1 Between friends

Work in pairs.

Pair A: You were recently given a job in a travel agency. A friend of yours, who applied for a job in the same travel agency, has just been rejected. You are surprised, because you think that he is better qualified than you are. His English is better, and he has spent more time living in England than you have. He is also a much more sociable and charming person than you; you are rather shy, and you're surprised you got through the interview yourself. You want to cheer him up by pointing out all his good qualities, and expressing your surprise that he didn't get the job.
Work out what you will say to him.

Pair B: You have just heard that your application for a job in a travel agency has been rejected. A friend of yours was recently accepted for a job in the same travel agency. You're disappointed, but you hadn't really expected to get the job, because you're not as well qualified as your friend. His English is better, and he's visited more foreign countries than you have. He also has a much more serious attitude to life than you; you think you may have given the impression of being too frivolous in the interview.
You know that your friend will be surprised that you didn't get the job, because he's very modest. You want to spare him any embarrassment by explaining why you think he got the job and you didn't.
Work out what you will say when A tries to cheer you up.

Now form new pairs and improvise the conversation.

C2 Who's who?

'Why, that's terrific! The subtlety of colour is unbelievable. And how did you manage to catch that mysterious smile? Wonderful! And well worth the 10,000 lire. My wife'll be delighted!'

1 Can you name the person being admired?
2 Now choose another famous person, alive or dead, and admire him/her, face to face, in the same way. Give enough clues (but not too many) so that his/her identity can be guessed.

Unit 5 Irritation/Impatience

Part one: Talking about the feeling

SECTION A: LISTENING AND DISCUSSION

A1 *Eve: . . .tap. . .tap. . .tap. . .*
Sue: Hmm! (cough)
Eve: . . .tap. . .tap. . .tap. . .
Sue: Hey, stop doing that, can't you? I'm trying to read!
Eve: . . .tap. . .tap. . .tap. . .
Sue: Did you hear what I said? Stop doing that!
Eve: . . .tap. . .tap. . .tap. . .
Sue: Oh, for goodness sake! Right, I'm going to the library!

A2 Facts

Discuss these questions.

1 Where do you think Eve and Sue are? In shared n or flat prop univ campus
2 Who do you think Eve and Sue are? Prob students. Rm or flates mates.
3 What is Eve doing? Tapping pens, fingers or table
4 What is Sue doing? Trying to read, study.
5 What does Sue want Eve to do? Wants to stop tapping.
6 How does Eve react? Ignores Sue keeps on
7 What does Sue do in the end? Walk out, slams door, goes library

A3 Language

Choose the best answers, and justify your choices. More than one answer may be right in each case.

1 Sue gets . . . . . .
   a) nervous. frightened
   b) annoyed.
   c) angry. little strong
   d) impatient. bit
   e) irritated.

38

2 Is Sue irritable?   *describes a ger characteristic the irritable person is one who*
       easily gets irritated of bad-tempered.
   a) Yes.   c) We can't be sure. –
   b) No.

3 Sue coughs to . . . . . . Eve's attention.
   a) draw   c) distract   *distract someone*
   b) attract   *draw someones attent to something*
                             to attract someones att, – to draw atter to yourself

4 Eve is . . . . . . Sue.
   a) distracting   c) disturbing   *distract – stop someone concentrating.*
   b) interrupting   *disturb – Annoy someone breaking into what doing*
                           b : break into conversat or work by talking

5 Eve is . . . . . . on the table.
   a) knocking   c) banging
   b) tapping   *a + c too loud*

6 Eve . . . . . . Sue.
   a) takes no notice of   c) doesn't take any notice of
   b) ignores   d) doesn't notice *– doesn't ser*

7 In the end, Sue can't . . . . . . it any longer.
   a) take   c) stand   *a) v. colloquial*
   b) carry   d) bear   *b) carry would have literal meaning*

SECTION B: PRACTICE

B1 Most annoying

'John was so *impatient* whenever he came round to take me out – I never had time to finish putting on my make-up. And I was *annoyed* by the way he bit his fingernails all the time. And the way he always talked about himself – I found that very *irritating*. I'd avoid him if I were you. . .'

1 What is the difference between *impatient, annoyed* and *irritated*?
2 Now talk about how Alan and Alice feel in the situations below. Use appropriate expressions from the list:

irritated	with someone		impatient	with someone
annoyed	by something			to do something
	by the way. . .			

   a) Alan wants to go out, but Alice is taking a long time getting ready.   *impatient*
   b) Alan's girlfriend keeps giggling.   *ann/irr*
   c) Alice is waiting for an interview for a job. She arrived on time, but has been waiting to go in for an hour.   *imp + ann/irr*
   d) Alan is in a hurry to get home, but the driver in front of him is driving very slowly.   *imp + ann/irr*
   e) Alice's mother keeps telephoning her to make sure she's all right.   *ann/irr*
   f) Alice still hasn't heard whether she's passed her exams or not.   *imp.*

B2 Story line

These expressions mean 'to continue doing. . .' or 'not to stop doing. . .':
to keep on doing. . .
to carry on doing. . .
to go on doing. . .

Look at the example, and then make similar reports from the notes below. Use the expressions in italics in your answers.

Example

RUDE PEOPLE: restaurant/man reading newspaper/'Is this seat free?'
Report: 'Aren't people rude nowadays! I went into a restaurant yesterday, and there was a man sitting at a table reading a newspaper. There was an empty seat next to him. I asked him if it was free, but he *ignored/didn't take any notice of/took no notice of* me. He just *kept on/carried on/went on* reading his newspaper.'

1 BAD SERVICE: cafe/waiters playing cards/'Can I have a cup of coffee, please?'
2 RUDE CHILDREN: street/children playing/'Can you tell me the way to King Sreet, please?'
3 UNFRIENDLY STAFF: office/secretary typing/'Could I see Mr Lang, please?'
4 INCONSIDERATE NEIGHBOURS: bed/man next door playing piano/Bang! Bang!
5 SELFISH PARENTS: sitting room/father watching BBC/'Can I watch the other channel, Dad?'

Delaying tactics p 44.

SECTION C: REPORTING

C1 Imagine that Sue is telling a friend about what happened.
How might she use the following expressions?

fed up   to disturb
to get on someone's nerves   to prevent
to concentrate   in the end/eventually

C2 Now imagine that you are Sue telling a friend about what happened. Write a report, using the language you have practised where you think it is appropriate.

Part two: Expressing the feeling

SECTION A: RECOGNITION

A1 Sweet or sour?

Look at the remarks below, and suggest situations in which they might be said.

1 I've told you twice already – five to four.
2 Go on then – overtake him.
3 I'm quite capable of finding my own way, thank you.
4 No, not 'persons' – 'people, people'.
5 Oh, I give up. See if you can undo it.
6 Oh darling, you know that I love you.
7 All right. I'll be down in a minute.
8 O.K., I'll take you home, if that's what you want.

"Try to get it right this time—I'll smile just once more!"

A2 Waiting list

Here are some expressions you might use when you are impatient to do something or get something:

I was wondering whether. . .yet.
I was wondering whether you'd mind. . .–ing. . .
I don't want to rush you but. . .
When are you going to. . .?
I suppose you couldn't. . ., could you?
I suppose you haven't. . ., have you?
Isn't it about time. . .?
Have/Has. . .yet?
What's happened to. . .?

Which could you use, without giving offence, in the following situations?

a) You are in a hurry to buy a train ticket. The person in front of you is wasting time by asking the ticket clerk for information about trains.

b) You have ordered a book at a bookshop. You need the book badly, so you call in at the shop to find out if it has come in.

c) A long time ago, a friend borrowed a dictionary from you. You expected him to return it weeks ago. You need it badly, so when you see him, you ask him about it.

SECTION B: PRACTICE

B1 Victimisation

Cacofonix, the bard, is singing his new composition. Here are some things that his friends say to him:

Asterix:	*Do you have to* play that horrible tune?
Obelix:	*I wish you wouldn't* sing that awful song!
Getafix:	*Stop* sing*ing* that terrible song, *will you?*
Vitalstatistix:	Put that lyre away, *can't you?*
Academix:	*Why do you keep* mak*ing* that awful noise?
Appliedlinguistix:	*I wish you'd* be quiet!

Work in groups.
One student: Do any of the irritating things in the list below.
The others: Show your irritation, using the expressions in italics above. Carry on until he stops!
Change roles from time to time.

scratch your head	suck your pencil	look at your watch
cough	yawn	tap on the desk
write	mutter to yourself	stare at the ceiling
stare at someone	hum a tune	look out of the window

B2 Wishful thinking

Here are some things that people might say to each other if they're both getting impatient:

I wish. . .
I wonder. . .
It's about time. . .

. . .ought to (have) | . . .by now.
. . .ago.

When do you think. . .?
. . .taking a long time to. . .
How much longer. . .?

Work in pairs.
1 Improvise more two-line conversations like those in the pictures. Use any of the expressions listed above.
2 Now imagine you're in the following situations. Improvise similar conversations. Make sure you cover the whole range of expressions.

   a) You're waiting to go into a shop, but it's still closed.
   b) You've sent your typewriter away to be repaired, and you're waiting to get it back.
   c) You're listening to a very long, boring speech.
   d) You're in a restaurant. Your meal is a long time coming.
   e) The skiing season has started, but there's no snow yet.
   f) You're in a plane, waiting for it to take off.

B3   Beauty and the Beasts

Beauty is at a party. Beast number 1 approaches her and offers her a drink. She refuses politely at first, but he is persistent and she gets annoyed. Here are some of the expressions she might use in her replies:

Beast: . . . . . .
Beauty: No thanks. I . . . . . .
Beast: . . . . . .
Beauty: | No, really. I . . . . . .
          | No, I really don't . . . . . .
          | No, honestly, I . . . . . .
          | No, I'm quite sure I don't . . . . . . |
Beast: . . . . . .
Beauty: | Look. I've already told you – I . . . . . .
          | Look. I've told you twice already – I . . . . . .
          | Look. How many times do I have to tell you – I . . . . . . |
          | Look. If I wanted . . . . . . |
Beast: . . . . . .
Beauty: | Oh, really! | I do wish you'd stop bothering me!
          | Oh, for goodness sake! |

1 a) Think of excuses that Beauty might give, and complete her replies.
   b) What do you think Beast might say at each stage?
   c) In pairs, act out the conversation.

2 Work in pairs.
   Improvise the conversations Beauty and the Beasts may have in these situations:

   a) Beast number 2 comes along and asks Beauty to dance.
   b) Beast number 3 comes along and asks Beauty to go for a walk in the garden.
   c) Beast number 4 comes along and asks Beauty to marry him.

SECTION C: FREE EXPRESSION

C1   Delaying tactics

Work in pairs.
Choose one of the following situations. Read the instructions for student A and student B below and improvise a conversation.

1 A is writing a thesis, which is due to be handed in in three days' time. B offered to type the thesis, but hasn't even started it yet. A telephones B, to remind him how urgent it is. B makes a lot of vague promises, but is unwilling to commit himself to a firm date.
2 A is out for a walk in the country, and wants to have lunch in a pub before closing time. He sees B, a local farmer, and asks him the way to the nearest pub. B tells A all about the pubs in the area, but keeps going off the point.
3 A is going on holiday to a foreign country, and realises at the last moment that he

needs a visa. He goes to the Consulate and asks B, a Consulate official, for a visa. B
is rather self-important, and makes everything seem more difficult than it really is.

Student A: You're in a hurry, but to get what you want you depend on B. Show
that you're impatient, but try not to offend B.

Student B: Use any means you can think of to avoid giving a straight answer. Go on
as long as you can without actually making A lose his temper.

C2 Do not disturb

Greta is baby-sitting. She is watching a very interesting television programme.
Madeleine, aged 6, keeps asking silly questions about it, and eventually Greta begins
to get irritated.

Madeleine: Greta, who's that man?
Greta: He's a detective, darling.
Madeleine: What's a detective?
Greta: He's a man who catches bad men.
Madeleine: Why's he got such a funny voice?
Greta: Oh, I don't know – because he's eating a lollipop probably.
Madeleine: Why's he eating a lollipop?
Greta: Because he's hun. . .Look – why don't you stop talking and just watch
the programme?
Madeleine: Greta, why hasn't he got any hair?
Greta: Oh, really! I do wish you'd stop asking silly questions. Go and play in the
garden or something, can't you?

What programme are they watching?
Now choose a television programme and write or improvise a similar conversation
between Greta and Madeleine.
Give enough information (but not too much) so that it is possible to guess the name
of the programme.

Unit 6 Delight/Relief

Part one: Talking about the feeling

SECTION A: LISTENING AND DISCUSSION

 A1 *Maisy: Er. . .do you have any plans for the summer?*
Clare: The summer? Well. . .um. . .
Maisy: The thing is, Cuthbert and I are going to Nice, and, well, we
were wondering if you and Tony. . .
Clare: Well, actually, I think Tony's arranged for us to. . .
Maisy: Oh, what a pity. You see, we were thinking you might like to
have our place in Cornwall while we're away. . .
Clare: Oh, Maisy. That is kind of you!. . .Well, yes. Of course. We'd
love to.
Maisy: Oh, good. I know how Tony enjoys gardening. . .

A2 Facts

Discuss these questions.

1 What is the relationship between Maisy and Clare?
2 'We were wondering if you and Tony. . .' How does Clare think Maisy is going to continue?
3 Why does Clare say 'I think Tony's arranged for us to. . .'?
4 What are Clare's plans for the summer?
5 What does Maisy offer Clare?
6 Why?

A3 Language

Choose the best answers, and justify your choices. More than one answer may be right in each case.

1 When Maisy asks Clare about her plans, Clare. . . . . .
  a) waits.
  b) hesitates.
  c) pauses.

2 She begins to tell Maisy that they . . . . . . for the summer.
  a) have made plans   c) have made arrangements
  b) have engagements

3 When Maisy offers to let her use the house, Clare is absolutely . . . . . .
  a) thrilled.   d) glad.
  b) delighted.   e) pleased.
  c) overjoyed.

4 Maisy is very . . . . . . that Clare wants to stay in her house.
  a) glad   d) pleased
  b) delighted   e) thrilled
  c) overjoyed

5 They are both . . . . . . with the way things have turned out.
  a) glad   c) pleased
  b) happy   d) satisfied

SECTION B: PRACTICE

B1 Good news

James has just passed his university entrance exam. Three people hear the news:

John says: 'Oh, good.'
Jack says: 'Oh, how marvellous!'
Jill says: 'Thank heavens for that!'

Which of them do you think is:

a) *relieved* (to hear) that James has got a place?
b) *delighted* (to hear) that James has got a place?
c) *pleased* (to hear) that James has got a place?
d) *glad* (to hear) that James has got a place?

Now talk about the following people, using the most appropriate expression from the above list in each case.

1 Andrew: 'Hello, Peter. I haven't seen you for a long time.'
2 Ben: 'At last! Another human being! You don't know what this means to me!'
3 Anna: 'You're quite sure he's safe? Ah, that's all right, then.'
4 Moira: 'Good old United! I knew they'd win!'
5 Vera: 'Mm. A postcard from Sue. That's nice of her.'
6 George: 'Thank goodness. I thought he was going to stay all night!'

▶ How could Maisy and Clare use this language to talk about what happened?

B2 Story line

Look at the example, and then make similar reports from the notes below. Use the expressions in italics in your answers.

Example

Later

Smythe: The Director called me into his office yesterday. *For a moment I* $\begin{vmatrix} thought \\ was\ afraid \end{vmatrix}$ he was going to give me the sack. But $\begin{vmatrix} it\ turned\ out\ that \\ as\ it\ turned\ out \end{vmatrix}$ he wanted to promote me. Of course, I was *absolutely* $\begin{vmatrix} delighted. \\ thrilled. \end{vmatrix}$ I just couldn't believe my luck. . .

Director: I called young Smythe into my office yesterday to tell him about his promotion. He looked *rather* $\begin{vmatrix} nervous \\ worried \end{vmatrix}$ when he came in. $\begin{vmatrix} I\ expect\ he\ thought \\ He\ must\ have\ thought \end{vmatrix}$ I was going to complain about something. Of course, when I told him, he was *absolutely* $\begin{vmatrix} delighted. \\ thrilled. \end{vmatrix}$ He couldn't thank me enough. . .

1 Friend: 'Would you like to come to a party?'
2 Father: 'I've bought you a new record-player.'
3 Bank Manager: 'You've inherited £1,000.'

Now think up a situation of your own.

▶ How could Maisy and Clare use this language to talk about what happened?

SECTION C: REPORTING

C1   Imagine that either Maisy or Clare is telling her husband about what happened. How might they use the following expressions?

taken aback   embarrassed
to get out of   to accept
awkward   relief

C2   Now imagine that you are either a) Maisy or b) Clare, telling your husband about what happened. Write a report, using the language you have practised where you think it is appropriate.

Part two: Expressing the feeling

SECTION A: RECOGNITION

 A1   **Feeling fine**

Look at the following remarks, and suggest situations in which they are appropriate.

1   And I should like to thank all of you who turned out in such large numbers today to give me their support.
2   Mm. . .68?. . .No, 69 – an exceptionally good year!
3   See? Told you it would turn cold!
4   Ah, that's better! Same again, please.
5   There we are – good as new!
6   Yes, and what about the bit where he drops the roast duck on the floor – I nearly died!
7   Encore!
8   Oh, yes! They'll never guess that one!

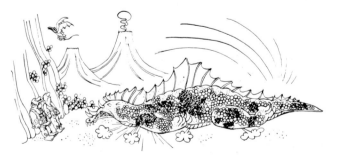

'Thank goodness! Extinct just in the nick of time!'

A2 Hello ... goodbye

Look at the pairs of remarks below, which are the opening and closing remarks of a conversation. Both remarks are made by the same person in each case. Who are the people? And what has happened during their conversation?

1 Fancy seeing you here. . .
 . . .It was good to see you again.
2 Pleased to meet you. . .
 . . .I'm glad to have had the opportunity of talking to you.
3 I'm so glad you could get here. . .
 . . .It was good of you to come all this way.
4 So glad you could come. . .
 . . .Nice having you.
5 Ah. Just the person I wanted to see. . .
 . . .Good. Eight o'clock, then.
6 Let's have a big hand for. . .
 . . .It was a pleasure to have you here tonight.
7 Of course. I'd be delighted. . .
 . . .Not at all. It was a pleasure.

SECTION B: PRACTICE

B1 What a relief

A B *Later*

1 Which of these remarks could fill the space in picture A, and which could fill the space in picture B?

  a) Thank goodness! We've got the harvest in!
  b) Thank goodness we've got the harvest in!
  c) Phew! I'm glad we've got the harvest in!
  d) Phew! We've got the harvest in at last!
  e) It's just as well we've got the harvest in!

f) It's lucky we've got the harvest in!

g) It's a good thing we've got the harvest in!

2 What do you think the people in these pictures might be saying? Make two sentences for each, as in the pictures of the farmers.

B2   A narrow escape

1 a) What has just happened? What very nearly happened?

b) What different things do you think the onlookers might be saying?

2 Work in groups.
Imagine that you are in one of the following situations. Express your relief, and speculate on what might have happened. Use the expressions above to help you.

a) You have just seen a lorry skid off the road, crash through a fence into a school playground, and stop within inches of the school wall. Fortunately it's Sunday, and the school is empty.

b) You all planned to book a skiing holiday through Con-Tours, a well-known package tour company. You happened to meet Fred, and old friend of yours, who told you they were very unreliable, so you decided not to go. Later you read that the company has collapsed, and that everyone who has booked a holiday with them has lost his money.

c) While you are having dinner, you realise that you have forgotten to bring in the mustard. You go to the kitchen to get it, and find that the stove has been left on, and that a frying pan full of oil has just caught fire.

d) You are visiting your friend Alex. He has just gone out shopping, and you are about to have a drink from a gin bottle you noticed in his kitchen. Alex comes back because he has forgotten his wallet, and tells you just in time that it contains a poisonous paint-remover.

B3 The perfect present

'I thought you could do with one of these.'   'I've got a little surprise for you.'

THROW-AWAY
LIGHTER
99 p.

GOLD LIGHTER
£ 120

'Mm. Thanks. That'll come in handy.'
'For me? That's very thoughtful of you.'

'Oh, how kind of you. That's just what I need.'
'Oh, very nice. I've always wanted one of those.'
'Ooh. A lighter. Thank you very much.'

'Oh, it's beautiful. Are you sure?'
'Is that really for me? It must've cost you a fortune!'
'What a lovely present! That *is* kind of you.'
'Oh, how can I ever thank you? It's just what I've always wanted.'
'Ooh, John! You shouldn't have!'

1 Which of these expressions might you use if a friend gave you:

   a) a bottle of wine
   b) a portable TV set
   c) £500
   d) a saucepan
   e) a matchbox-holder in the shape of the Leaning Tower of Pisa.

2 Work in groups.
Write down on pieces of paper the names of some things you might give as presents.
Give the 'presents' to each other.

SECTION C: FREE EXPRESSION

C1 Summer course

Work in pairs.
Pair A: You are attending a summer course at the Anglophile School of English in a seaside town in England. You're enjoying yourself very much – you like the classes, you find the town attractive, and you're meeting a lot of students from different countries. You're staying with an English family, and you practise your English as much as possible with your landlady; and there are plenty of pubs and parties to go to in the evenings.
It's a beautiful morning. You feel so good that you want to tell everybody how happy you are. At coffee break, another student comes and sits at your table.
Work out what your will say to him/her.
Pair B: You are attending a summer course at the Anglophile School of English in a seaside town in England. You're not having a particularly good time – the teaching methods are unfamiliar, you've hardly met any English people except your landlady, and you think the town is rather ordinary. You don't like living with a family, because this restricts your freedom, and in any case you haven't found much to do in the evenings except going to pubs and parties with the same old people.
For once, the weather's quite nice, and you wish you didn't have any lessons. You're feeling a bit fed up. At coffee break you sit down next to another student and start talking to him/her.
Work out what you will say to him/her.

Now form new pairs and improvise the conversation.

C2   Having a lovely time. . .

ITALY · THE ALPS · THE COUNTRY · THE CARIBBEAN · GERMANY

an old lady
a poet
a millionaire
a teenager
a professor

Choose one of the people and one of the holidays. Write a postcard to a friend, saying how much you are enjoying yourself. Give enough clues (but not too many) so that it is possible to guess:

a) which of the people you are.
b) which holiday you are on.

Unit 7 Indignation/Annoyance

Part one: Talking about the feeling

SECTION A: LISTENING AND DISCUSSION

A1
Clive: *Another half, please.*
Daniel: *Sorry, sir. Time's been called.*
Clive: *Oh, you needn't worry about that.*
Daniel: *I'm afraid I have to, sir.*
Clive: *I see. What about those two over there, then? They seem to be...*
Daniel: *Ah, but they're residents, sir.*
Clive: *Residents? What do you mean, residents? Friends of the landlord, more likely!...Bloody cheek!*
Daniel: *'Night, sir.*

A2 Facts

Discuss these questions.
1 What is the relationship between Clive and Daniel?
2 Where are they?
3 What does Clive want?
4 How does Daniel react, and why?
5 What are the residents doing?
6 Why is Clive treated differently from them?
7 What does Clive think is going on?
8 What does Clive do in the end?

A3 Language

Choose the best answers, and justify your choices. More than one answer may be right in each case.

1 Clive seems to be . . . . . . type of person.
  a) a touchy   d) a bad-tempered
  b) a moody   e) a quick-tempered
  c) an angry

2 When Daniel refuses to serve him, Clive gets . . . . . .
   a) irritated.   d) excited.
   b) annoyed.   e) indignant.
   c) displeased.

3 By the end, Clive is . . . . . .
   a) very angry.   c) absolutely angry.
   b) very furious.   d) absolutely furious.

4 Clive . . . . . . Daniel's attitude.
   a) dislikes   d) is displeased with
   b) resents   e) is unhappy about
   c) objects to

5 Clive finds Daniel . . . . . .
   a) infuriating.   c) distressing.
   b) offensive.

6 Clive . . . . . . treating him unfairly.
   a) accuses Daniel for   c) blames Daniel for
   b) accuses Daniel of   d) blames Daniel of

7 As he goes out, Clive . . . . . . Daniel.
   a) swears   c) curses
   b) swears at   d) curses at

SECTION B: PRACTICE

B1 Bad feeling

You're *annoyed* if you're slightly angry.
You're *furious* if you're very angry indeed.

Hurt   Offended   Indignant
June, Janet and Jasmine all expected to be invited to their friend Jenny's wedding, but none of them got an invitation.

June was *hurt*:
'I do think she might have invited me', she said, almost crying, and felt miserable all day.

Janet was *offended*:
'That's no way to treat a friend', she said, and decided not to send Jenny a card.

Jasmine was *indignant*:
'Who does she think she is, ignoring me like that?' she screamed, and immediately wrote a letter demanding an explanation.

You can only be *hurt* or *offended* by people behaving badly towards you.
You can be *indignant* about anything you disapprove of, whether it affects you or not
e.g. Josie is indignant about animals being used for scientific experiments.

1 Which of the people above could also be *angry* or *furious?*
2 Look at the remarks below, and make a sentence, using the best word in the list, to describe the feelings of the speaker in each case.
annoyed
indignant
hurt
offended

   a) What a nuisance, having this cold.
   b) Look here, you can't arrest me! Take your hands off me!
   c) All right, so you think I'm a fool.
   d) Oh Jenny, if you really loved me, you wouldn't have said that. . .
   e) Attacking a defenceless old lady! The hooligans! They ought to be locked up!
   f) Hey, watch where you're going – you almost spilt my drink.
   g) I'm very surprised that you're dissatisfied, sir. Most of our guests find the beds very comfortable.

▶ How could Clive and Daniel use this language to talk about what happened?

B2 Story line

SORRY, WE'RE DELIVERING SOMETHING NEXT DOOR.

1 Decide what is happening in the picture. Then tell the story from the point of view of a) the car driver, b) the lorry driver, using the expressions in the lists.

Car driver	*Lorry driver*
. . .I asked him. . .	. . .He wanted/asked me. . .
. . .he refused to/wouldn't. . .	. . .I told him I couldn't. . .
. . .made some (feeble) excuse about. . .	. . .tried to explain. . .
. . .made me absolutely furious/really annoyed me. . .	. . .lost his temper/got most indignant. . .
. . .told him (exactly) what I thought of him. . .	. . .started shouting/swearing at me. . .

2 Now make similar reports for these pictures:

▶ How could Clive and Daniel use this language to talk about what happened?

SECTION C: REPORTING

C1 Imagine that Clive or Daniel is telling a friend about what happened. How might they use the following expressions?

to point out	argumentative
closing time	to take offence
to insist	to storm out
off-hand	

C2 Now imagine that you are either a) Clive or b) Daniel, telling a friend about what happened. Write a report, using the language you have practised where you think it is appropriate.

Part two: Expressing the feeling

SECTION A: RECOGNITION

A1 All steamed up

Look at the following remarks, in which people are expressing indignation, and suggest situations in which they might be appropriate.

1 Bird-watching indeed! And that's a camera you've got there, I suppose!
2 It's not as if he was hard up, after all.

3 Call this tidy? You ought to be ashamed of yourself!
4 You'll never get away with this.
5 Lives before lorries!
6 Can't you be serious for once?
7 All right, that'll do. . .That'll do, I said!
8 Well, all I can say is, don't come running to me!
9 What do you mean, *your* book?

"What do you mean, no?"

A2 Going to extremes

That does it!
How dare you!
Have it your own way!
I *beg* your pardon!
Now look what you've done!
What do you think you're doing?
What do you mean?
That's all I need!
All right, if that's the way you feel about it!

Which of the above expressions would you use in these situations?

a) Someone has just accused you of stealing something.
b) You see someone trying the door of your car.
c) Someone refuses to listen to your advice.
d) Someone who's accidentally broken two of your best plates already has just dropped a third.

59

SECTION B: PRACTICE

B1 Finding fault

It's all your fault (that). . .
It's all your fault for. . .–ing. . .
You should/shouldn't have. . .
If you had/hadn't. . .
It was you that. . . (not me).

1 a) Why do you think John and Mary are late for the theatre?
   b) Think of some of the things they might say to each other outside the theatre. Use the expressions listed above.
   c) Think of some expressions they might use to deny each other's accusations.
   d) In pairs, improvise John and Mary's conversation.

2 Work in pairs.
   a) Look at the pictures below. Decide what is happening, what the people in them might have been doing, and how they got into the situation they are in.
   b) For each picture improvise a dialogue between the two people, in which they blame each other for what has happened.

B2 What a nerve!

Airport shock: 'We weren't consulted' say angry villagers

MANWICKSHIRE County Council yesterday approved Government plans to build a second airport to serve the city of Manwick. The proposed site for the airport is 20 miles west of the city, only a few miles from the historic village of Whimsy.

There was a storm of protest in the village when the decision was announced yesterday. In an interview on Manwick radio last night, Mr Albert Crankshaw, president of the Whimsy Residents' Association, said 'We are appalled. This decision will mean the end of Whimsy. Planes will be taking off and coming in to land directly over the village...'

1 What different things do you think the people in the pub might be indignant about?

Complete their remarks.

2 Work in groups.
   a) Together, choose a topic you all feel indignant about.
   b) Individually, or in pairs, make notes on
       i) things that are happening that you don't like
       ii) things you think should be happening.
   c) Get together again and talk about it. Be as indignant as you can.

B3 Broken promises

Paul and Dave are flat-mates. On Saturday morning, Paul promised to get in a lot of food for the weekend. When Dave came home in the evening, he found that Paul hadn't bought anything. Here is part of their conversation:

Dave:
> You said you'd . . . . . .
> You promised you'd . . . . . .
> What happened to . . . . . .?
> Why didn't you . . . . . .?
> I thought you were going to . . . . . .

Paul: . . . . . .

Dave:
> I see. You might (at least) have . . . . . .
> Well. You could (at least) have . . . . . .
> Hmm. Surely you could have . . . . . .

Paul: . . . . . .

Dave: Huh!
> Trust you to . . . . . .
> Just like you to . . . . . .
> If there's one thing that annoys me, it's people who . . . . . .

1 a) Complete Dave's remarks.
   b) What excuses might Paul make?
   c) In pairs, act out the conversation between Dave and Paul.

2 Work in pairs.
   Imagine you are in these situations, and improvise similar conversations, using suitable expressions from above.

   a) Paul went abroad for a holiday, and promised to write a long letter, but didn't.
   b) Paul promised to introduce Dave to a girl he knew, but didn't.
   c) Paul promised to clean up the flat, but didn't.
   d) Dave went away, and his brother came to stay in the flat for a week. Paul promised to entertain him and show him round, but didn't.
   e) Dave agreed to let Paul get a cat, provided he looked after it properly. Paul promised he would, but didn't.
   f) Dave let Paul use his new hi-fi on condition he was very careful with it. Paul promised to be careful, but wasn't.

SECTION C: FREE EXPRESSION

C1 Dangerous drivers

Work in pairs.

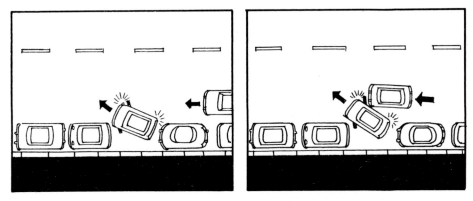

Pair A: You were looking for a place to park. You saw a driver signalling that he
was going to pull out, and you slowed down so that you could occupy his
space when he moved away.
However, he didn't move, so you decided to drive on and look for a space
further on. As you passed him, he pulled out and crashed into you.
Of course you think the accident was his fault. Work out what you will say
to him.

Pair B: Your car was parked by the side of the road. You got in, signalled that you
were going to move out, and looked to see if there were any cars coming.
You saw one car coming along the road, but the driver slowed down and
seemed to be waiting for you to go. You waited a moment to make sure that
he really was stopping, and then you pulled out. As you did so, he suddenly
speeded up, and crashed into you.
Of course you think the accident was his fault. Work out what you will say
to him.

Now form new pairs and improvise the conversation.

C2 More Manwick developments

Manwick City Council has decided to pull down the houses in Jubilee Street, near the
town centre, to make way for offices. They are going to rehouse the residents in
high-rise blocks in various suburbs. The people who live in Jubilee Street all know
each other very well, and they resent being moved out. They think that the Council
should make improvements to their houses instead of knocking them down.

Work in groups of five.

Group A: You are a reporter. In an interview for local radio you ask four of the
residents of Jubilee Street what they feel about the Council's decision.

Group B: You are Mr Phipps, aged 74. You have lived in Jubilee Street all your life.

Group C: You are Mrs Oakley, aged 35, mother of three.
Group D: You are Mr Wells, aged 50. You run the corner shop.
Group E: You are Angela Forbes, a writer. You came to live in Jubilee Street three
years ago.

1 In your groups, work out what you will say in the interview.
2 Form new groups and improvise the interview.

Unit 8 Surprise

Part one: Talking about the feeling

SECTION A: LISTENING AND DISCUSSION

A1 *David:* Excuse me, do you happen to know. . .Hey, I know you! It's Archie, isn't it?

Archie: David! It can't be! Fancy seeing you here!

David: Incredible! After all this time. . .

Archie: You're the last person I expected to meet out here. What are you doing here, anyway?

David: Oh, I've come out to work for UNESCO. An irrigation project, you know. I'll be taking over from some chap who's. . .wait a minute. . .Of course! Archie MacDonald! Now that is a coincidence!

A2 Facts

Discuss these questions.
1 What is the relationship between David and Archie?
2 Where do you think they are?
3 How long has each of them been there?
4 What do you think David's profession is?
   What job do you think he is about to take up?
5 How might his remark 'I'll be taking over from some chap who's. . .' continue?
6 Why does he say 'Wait a minute'?
7 Who is MacDonald?

A3 Language

Choose the best answers, and justify your choices. More than one answer may be right in each case.

1 David . . . . . . Archie quite unexpectedly.
  a) meets   c) goes into
  b) finds   d) runs into

65

2 David and Archie are . . . . . . to see each other.
   a) surprised   c) astonished
   b) shocked   d) amazed

3 They think it is . . . . . .coincidence.
   a) an unusual   d) a remarkable
   b) an extraordinary   e) an incredible
   c) an unlikely

4 David doesn't . . . . . .Archie immediately.
   a) realise   c) remember
   b) recognise

5 David is . . . . . . MacDonald.
   a) changing places with   c) replacing
   b) working with

6 Suddenly he . . . . . . that he's taking over from Archie.
   a) realises   c) learns
   b) recognises   d) thinks

SECTION B: PRACTICE

B1 Surprising news

Alex, Arthur and Andrew have just heard that the President has resigned.

Alex was *surprised to* hear the news.
It came as quite *a surprise* to him.
'Oh, really?' he said. 'I didn't expect that to happen.'

Arthur was $\begin{vmatrix} astonished \\ amazed \end{vmatrix}$ *to* hear the news.

It came as a great surprise to him.
'What? I don't believe it!' he said. 'He can't have done!'

Andrew was *shocked to* hear the news.
It came as a great *shock* to him.
'Oh no! How dreadful!' he said. 'What a terrible thing to happen!'

1 What is the difference between *surprised, astonished, amazed* and *shocked*?
2 Imagine that you experienced these things. Say how you reacted, giving two sentences for each answer.
   a) You heard on the news that train fares were going up.
   b) Your brother was made Prime Minister.
   c) You read in a newspaper that oil had been discovered in Central London.
   d) A friend of yours learnt to speak fluent Hungarian in three weeks.
   e) Your sister's marriage broke up.
   f) The flowers came out in your garden in January.
   g) A friend who you'd been out of touch with for years sent you a birthday card.

▶ How could David use this language to talk about what happened?

B2 Story line

Look at the example, then make similar reports from the headlines below. Use the expressions in italics where appropriate.

Example: SECRETARY MEETS BOSS IN DISCOTHEQUE
Report: 'I went to the Spot Discotheque last night. After I'd been there a short

time, *I was* | surprised / astonished / amazed | *to* | see / find / discover | that my boss was there too – dancing

wildly in a dark corner. *I could hardly believe my eyes* when I saw him – I

mean,   he *was the last* person *I'd expected to* meet.'
                 it *was the last* thing *I'd expected to* happen.'

  1 MARS EXPEDITION DISCOVERS GIANT MUSHROOMS
  2 HOUSEWIFE SEES UNICORN IN BACK GARDEN

  3 STUDENT WINS £5,000 ON FOOTBALL POOLS
  4 FREAK SUMMER SNOWFALL IN MADRID

Now think up a headline of your own and make a report.

▶ How could David use this language to talk about what happened?

SECTION C: REPORTING

C1 Imagine that David is writing a letter to his wife about what happened. How might he use the following expressions?

coincidence   to dawn on
to have no idea   to connect
to happen to

C2 Now imagine that you are David, writing to your wife about what happened. Writ the part of the letter that describes the incident, using the language you have practise where you think it is appropriate.

Part two: Expressing the feeling

SECTION A: RECOGNITION

 A1 **Surprise surprise**

Suggest situations in which the remarks below might be said, and what they might be replies to.

1 Haven't you? That's funny. I've caught dozens.
2 I say, that was quick. I've only got to line 10.
3 What? He can't be! I've only just given him his breakfast.
4 Really?. . .Oh, no!. . .Did you really?. . .Mm. . .You must have been, yes.
5 Well, well! Fancy giving it to him! With his accent!
6 But that's ridiculous! After all he's done for the village!
7 Good Lord! You're right – it *is* our house!
8 What, for me? I wonder who it is.
9 What on earth did you move there for?. . .Oh, no!

*"She's not **my** aunt! . . . I thought she was **your** aunt!"*

A2 In a manner of speaking

'Oh no, you didn't, did you?'

On the tape you will hear this remark made in five different ways. Which one could be a reply to:

a) Look – I'm sorry, but I'm afraid I burnt rather a large hole in your Persian carpet.
b) . . .so I called all the neighbours together and persuaded them to march to the Town Hall in protest.
c) Guess who I met last night – Susan Smiles!
d) I keep telling you – I never went to Naples.
e) The interview? Well, to tell you the truth, I made a complete mess of it.

Which of the replies express only surprise, and which express other feelings as well?

SECTION B: PRACTICE

B1 False impressions

1 What might the people in the pictures say instead of 'How extraordinary!'?
2 Which of the expressions in the list might the person in picture 1 use? Which of them might the person in picture 2 use?

   a) Who would've thought. . .?
   b) I didn't know. . .
   c) I was sure. . .
   d) I could have sworn. . .
   e) I was quite certain. . .
   f) I never expected. . .

3 Use the expressions to make further captions for pictures 1 and 2.

4 Now make captions for these pictures:

B2 Tall stories

Gerry: Guess what. I've just won £1,000.

Jean:
| You haven't!
| You haven't, have you?
| Have you really?
| What? You can't have done!
| £1,000? I don't believe it!

Gerry: Yes, and what's more, the Queen's going to present me with the cheque!

Jean:
| She isn't!
| She isn't, is she?
| Is she really?
| What? She can't be!
| The Queen? I don't believe it!

1 In pairs, improvise similar four-line conversations starting with the following remarks.

   a) You'll never guess – I appeared on TV last night.
   b) Guess what. It's snowing outside.
   c) Have you heard? All the teachers are going on strike.
   d) You know what? I've just had a novel published.
   e) Did you know? The Beatles are together again.

2 Work in groups.
   Each student takes it in turn to say something surprising and/or unlikely. The others reply appropriately.

B3 Out of the blue

Pam: I've just had a letter from Richard. Apparently he's started going to keep-fit classes.

Sid:	Good Lord! Well, well! Good heavens!	How That's	amazing! incredible! extraordinary!	Whatever made him . . . . .? I wonder why he . . . . . .? What did he . . . . . . for? Why on earth . . . . . .?

Pam: . . . . . . Sid: Yes, but	even so still all the same	You would(n't) have thought he'd . . . . . . It seems strange that he should . . . . . . I never expected him to . . . . . . It's not like him to . . . . . .

Pam: Yes, it	does seem is	a bit	odd funny strange	doesn't it? isn't it?

1 a) Complete Pam's and Sid's remarks.
  b) In pairs, act out their conversation, and continue it in any way you like.

2 Work in pairs.
  Imagine that one of you has heard the following pieces of news about someone you both know. Improvise conversations, similar to the one above.

  a) Jim has just joined the army.
  b) Arthur and Emma have emigrated to Canada.
  c) Gregory has given up drinking.
  d) Your boss has decided to retire.
  e) Alice has decided to marry Ed.

SECTION C: FREE EXPRESSION

C1 Jude the Obscure

Work in groups of four.
You are old friends from university. You all knew Jude when he was a student, but none of you have seen him for several years. You have each heard different stories about what he's doing, and are very surprised when you hear what the others say about him.

Group A: You heard that
        – he had got a job in London in an insurance agency.
        – he had married a Spanish girl.
        – he had a holiday cottage in Scotland.

Group B: You heard that
        – he gave extravagant parties.
        – he had a beautiful Brazilian girlfriend.
        – he was studying in London.

Group C: You heard that
       – he had gone to live on a Scottish island.
       – he didn't let anyone visit him.
       – he had taken his Brazilian wife and baby with him.

Group D: You heard that
       – he was doing a PhD in Cambridge.
       – he was going out with an Italian girl.
       – he gave a lot of parties.

1 In your groups, work out a consistent story about Jude based on the notes above. Add details of your own.
2 Form new groups and talk about Jude. Speak in any order and interrupt each other when you hear something you don't think is true.

C2 Newsdesk

Here is one half of a telephone conversation. What is it about? What do you think the other person says?

'Hello. Newsdesk. . . Oh, yes? What was it?. . . A what? Where?. . .Are you sure it wasn't just a reflection of some kind?. . .Right over your house? Good Lord!. . .Men? What sort of men?. . .Good heavens!. . .A cup of *tea*? Surely not!. . .'

Think of a surprising piece of news that might be heard over the telephone at Newsdesk. Write down what the man at the newsdesk might say as he listens to the story.
Give enough clues (but not too many) so that it is possible to guess what the conversation is about.

Unit 9 Disappointment/Regret

Part one: Talking about the feeling

SECTION A: LISTENING AND DISCUSSION

A1 *Susan:* *I don't know, Cathy – things seem to be going from bad to worse. Sometimes I get the feeling that they. . .well, they just seem to take me so much for granted. If only I had a job or something – then at least I'd feel I was really doing something. . . Perhaps I shouldn't have got married in the first place. Then I could have got my degree, and who knows what I might be doing now. Not washing up, that's for sure.*

Cathy: *Well, you know, Susan, I did warn you. . .*

Susan: *Yes I know you did, Cath – but it all seemed so different then. How was I to know it'd turn out like this?*

A2 Facts

Discuss these questions.
1 What is the relationship between Susan and Cathy?
2 What is Susan's occupation?
3 How does she spend her time?
4 When did she get married?
5 What can you tell about her husband?
6 What might Cathy have told Susan before Susan got married?

A3 Language

Choose the best answers and justify your choices. More than one answer may be right in each case.

1 Susan is . . . . . . doing housework.
   a) tired of
   b) sick of
   c) fed up of
   d) tired with
   e) sick with
   f) fed up with

73

2 She is . . . . . . with being a housewife.
   a) disappointed   c) dissatisfied
   b) disillusioned

3 She feels that her husband and children don't . . . . . . her.
   a) like   c) appreciate
   b) want

4 She regrets . . . . . .
   a) getting married.   d) to have got married.
   b) to get married.   e) that she got married.
   c) having got married.

5 She wishes she . . . . . .
   a) wouldn't get married.   c) hasn't got married.
   b) didn't get married.   d) hadn't got married.

6 She wishes she . . . . . .
   a) has a job.   c) had a job.
   b) would have a job.   d) had had a job.

SECTION B: PRACTICE

B1   Feeling low

Jack had always wanted to be a sailor; he'd thought it would be a great life. But things didn't turn out very well:

He was *dissatisfied with* his pay and working conditions.
He *found* his pay and working conditions *unsatisfactory*.

He was *disappointed with* the places he visited.
He *found* the places he visited *disappointing*.

And he was | *tired of* / *sick of* / *fed up with* | cleaning the decks every day.

In fact, he was altogether *disillusioned with* being a sailor.

74

1 In your own words, explain how Jack felt about a) his pay and working conditions, b) the places he visited, c) cleaning the decks, and d) being a sailor.
2 Talk about the feelings of the people below, choosing the most appropriate expressions from the list.

dissatisfied	disappointed	tired of	disillusioned
unsatisfactory	disappointing	sick of	
		fed up with	

a) Thomas was 19, but he was still at school.
b) Everyone had said how funny the new film was, but Mary didn't laugh once.
c) Janet felt that she had achieved very little in her fifteen years as a social worker.
d) The miners went on strike for more pay.
e) Every Monday, Wednesday and Friday, Alf's wife brought home fish and chips for dinner.
f) Annabel had always imagined that caviare must be delicious – until she actually tried some.
g) As the war dragged on, Robert began to wonder what it was they were all fighting and dying for.

▶ How could Susan use this language to talk about what happened?

B2 Upsetting Events

Eve was very upset when Peter didn't send her a card on St Valentine's Day.

It was a great disappointment to her.
It came as a terrible disappointment to her.
She was dreadfully disappointed.

Eve was very upset when she heard that Peter was going out with other women.

It was a great shock to her.
It came as a dreadful shock to her.
It gave her a terrible shock.

Now talk about Peter in the following situations, using appropriate expressions from above.

1 Peter only got seven Valentine cards.
2 He heard that his best friend had been spreading nasty rumours about him.
3 He didn't do very well in his exams.
4 He was expelled from university.
5 Eve left him.

SECTION C: REPORTING

C1 Imagine you are writing a short story for a magazine about Susan. How might you use the following expressions?

to sigh
career
frustrated
routine
pointless
to drift apart

TRUE STORY OF THE WEEK

Love in Chains

'Susan sighed as her mind drifted back over five long years of married life . . .'

C2 Write a paragraph to begin the story, describing Susan's situation and her feelings about it.

Part two: Expressing the feeling

SECTION A: RECOGNITION

A1 What's wrong?

Look at the following remarks, and suggest situations in which they might be said.

1 Yes – pity about the music, though.
2 Hm. So much for Wonderflakes.
3 Yes, we might just as well have given them something out of a tin.
4 It's the garden I miss more than anything else.
5 Still engaged. Ah, well – at least we've tried.
6 Oh no! Just when we needed the money too!
7 Dentist?. . .Oh, my God! I knew there was something!
8 Oh no! Not more adverts!

"Damn it, and I went and bought today's".

A2 Life at the top

Look at this series of pictures. Then put the captions below in the order you think most appropriate (one for each picture).

1 I must have been crazy to move into a top floor flat.
2 Perhaps I shouldn't have moved into a top floor flat.
3 I simply can't think why I moved into a top floor flat.
4 I'm beginning to wish I hadn't moved into a top floor flat.
5 If only I hadn't moved into a top floor flat.

A3 Friday the thirteenth

13 Friday	13.00
09.00	14.00 *Reception at Embassy (black tie)*
10.00 *Appointment with bank manager*	15.00
11.00 *Council meeting*	16.00 *6.30 Drink with Archie (Red Lion)*
12.00 *12.30 Lunch with Mr + Mrs Sweeney*	17.00 *8.00 SUSIE (mustn't be late this time !!!)*

Phil had a busy timetable for Friday the thirteenth. Unfortunately, he woke up with a very high temperature, and was unable to get up for two days. When he was a bit better, he wrote letters of apology to all the people he had arranged to meet. Here are extracts from his six letters. Who do you think each one is addressed to?

a) Mr Richards regrets that owing to illness he was unable to be present on Friday.
b) You'll never forgive me for not turning up on Friday, but believe me it was impossible.
c) Sorry about Friday. I was ill.
d) I must apologise for not coming on Friday. I hope this didn't cause you too much inconvenience.
e) I'm very sorry I couldn't make it on Friday. I'm afraid I was ill.
f) I should like to apologise for not being able to attend on Friday, but I was suddenly taken ill.

SECTION B: PRACTICE

B1 One thing after another

A few days ago you had a row with your wife because you didn't want to lend her the car. You went out and got drunk, and forgot to set the alarm when you went to bed. Next morning you woke up with a terrible hangover, and got to work two hours late. You were in such a bad mood that when your boss asked you why you were late, you lost your temper and shouted at him. He gave you the sack, and you were so upset that you had a car accident on the way home. Later, in hospital, you begin to regret everything that happened.

1 What different things might you say to yourself? Fill in the gaps.

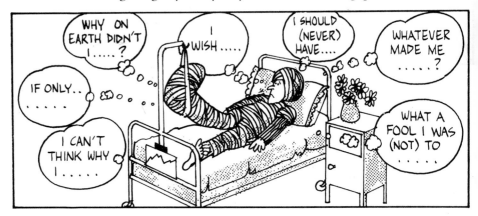

2 Look at the three pictures below. What do you think has happened? What are the people in them regretting?
What might the people in each picture be saying or thinking?

B2 What a let down

Here are some other expressions you can use when you're disappointed with something:

...wasn't $\begin{vmatrix} \text{up to much} \\ \text{much good} \end{vmatrix}$

...could have been better

...didn't think much of...

...wasn't as...as...

...wasn't worth...–ing...

1 How would you use these expressions to talk about 'Kung Fu Queen'?
2 In pairs, improvise more two-line conversations like those in the picture, using the expressions in the list.
3 Now imagine you are in the following situations. Improvise similar conversations. Make sure you cover the whole range of expressions.
   a) You've just had a steak in an expensive restaurant. It was a bit tough.
   b) You drove thirty miles to visit a famous cathedral, but found it very ordinary.
   c) You've just come back from a rather boring party.
   d) You went to a lecture on American Poetry by a famous professor. He had very little to say that you didn't know already.

B3 Manwick depression

Martin, a second-year student at the University of Manwick, is getting a bit disillusioned with university life: it isn't as stimulating as he had expected it to be. One morning, Carol sees him looking particularly gloomy, and asks him what the matter is.

Carol:
| What's up with you?
| What's up?
| What's wrong?
| What's the matter?

Martin:
| Oh, I don't know.
| Oh, nothing, really.

|| I'm just a bit fed up
|| I'm just a bit depressed
|| I'm just feeling a bit low
|| Things are getting me down a bit

| that's all.

Carol: . . . . . .

Martin: Oh, it's not that so much. It's . . . . . .
| I just don't seem to be able to . . . . . .
| Sometimes I get the feeling that . . . . . .
| I'm beginning to think/wonder. . . . . .

Carol: Oh, how's that?
Martin: . . . . . .

1 a) What do you think Carol's second remark might be?
   b) Complete Martin's replies.
   c) How do you think the conversation might continue?
   d) In pairs, act out the conversation between Carol and Martin. Continue in any way you like.

2 Work in pairs.
   Carol meets three other gloomy friends on the campus. Improvise similar conversations.
   a) Sarah, who is living in a very small flat which she shares with two other people.
   b) Nigel, who is involved in so many activities at the university that he never has a moment to himself.
   c) Heather, who is studying Greek Philosophy, and is finding it a bit baffling.
   d) Monique, who is living at home with her parents, and would like to be more independent.

SECTION C: FREE EXPRESSION

C1 Second thoughts

HAD ENOUGH OF THE RAT-RACE? Would you like to join a small community who are trying to find a less competitive and more peaceful way of life? We have bought a large old farm on the island of Skerry in the Hebrides, and need like-minded people with any practical skills who can make a real contribution to the community. No electricity. Lots of hard work. We aim to be self-sufficient. Box no. 412.

Three years after this advertisement appeared in *The Times,* a television crew visited Skerry to find out how well the community was surviving. They found that many of the people there were very disillusioned, and were thinking of leaving.

Work in groups of five.

Group A: You are a reporter. You interview four people to find out how they feel about life in the community.

Group B: You are Jim, a carpenter with a wife and two children.

Group C: You are Shirley. You went to the island after having got a degree in agriculture.

Group D: You are Gerald. You gave up your job as a primary school teacher to go and live in the community.

Group E: You are Miranda, a former art student. You and your husband were working in advertising before you joined the community.

1 In your groups, work out what you will say in the interview.
2 Form new groups and improvise the interview.

C2   A bad move

Here are six places to live. Imagine that you used to live in one, and that you have recently moved to another. You are not very happy in your new home and you wish you hadn't moved.
Write part of a letter to a friend, expressing your disappointment with your new home, and saying what you miss about your old one. Give enough clues (but not too many) so that it is possible to guess where you used to live, and where you live now.

Unit 10 Interest/Curiosity

Part one: Talking about the feeling

SECTION A: LISTENING AND DISCUSSION

A1 *Harry: Excuse me, I don't want to seem inquisitive, but um. . .what exactly are you doing?*

James: I'm recording things people say.

Harry: The things people say? What things?

James: Oh, anything – anything they happen to say.

Harry: Oh, I see. . .but why here, of all places?

James: Well, as a matter of fact, I'm making a study of the things people say on trains.

Harry: I say, what a fascinating idea! I've often wondered what people really say to each other on trains. Um. . .I don't suppose I could hear a bit of it, could I? It really does sound most interesting.

James: All right. Just a minute. . .here goes. . .

Voice: Excuse me, I don't want to seem inquisitive, but um. . .

A2 Facts

1 What is the relationship between Harry and James?
2 Where are Harry and James?
3 What is James holding?
4 What do you think James's occupation is?
5 What is James doing when he says 'Just a minute'?
6 What doesn't Harry realise until the end?

A3 Language

Choose the best answers and justify your choices. More than one answer may be right in each case.

1 Harry is . . . . . . to know what James is doing.
   a) interested   c) inquisitive
   b) curious

83

2 Harry's curiosity is . . . . . . by what James is doing.
   a) raised   c) lifted
   b) aroused

3 Harry is . . . . . . by what James is doing.
   a) interested   c) curious
   b) fascinated   d) intrigued

4 Harry is . . . . . . in what James is doing.
   a) interested   c) curious
   b) fascinated   d) intrigued

5 Harry doesn't want to appear . . . . . .
   a) interested.   d) inquisitive.
   c) curious.

6 James is . . . . . . to play the tape to Harry.
   a) happy   d) willing
   b) prepared   e) obliged
   c) wanting

SECTION B: PRACTICE

B1 Shades of interest

The stranger *interested* Emily.
Emily *found* the stranger *interesting*.
Emily *was interested by* (*in*) the stranger.

1 Look at the sentences below and
   a) Explain the meaning of *fascinated, intrigued* and *bored*.
   b) Supply the other two forms, as in the list above.

     Emily *was fascinated* by the stranger.
     (He was very charming. She couldn't take her eyes off him.)

     Emily *was intrigued* by the stranger.
     (He was very mysterious. She kept wondering who he could be.)

     Emily *was bored* by the stranger.
     (He talked so much that she nearly fell asleep.)

2 Use appropriate forms of *interest, bore, fascinate* and *intrigue* to talk about the
  following situations.

   a) When Michael came home from work, he found a large box on the doorstep.
   b) John enjoyed the lecture.
   c) Mary sat with her eyes glued to the little silver ball which was swinging to and
      fro in front of her face.

    d) Sam got a letter with his brother's handwriting on the envelope, postmarked 'New Guinea'.

    e) Elizabeth wished she had never agreed to go to the concert.

    f) The Prince stood, unable to move, listening to the beautiful song which drifted down from the small window high above him.

▶ How could Harry and James use this language to talk about what happened?

B2 Storyline

'Last Saturday was so hot that I decided to use my umbrella as a sunshade. People started staring at me.

They | *must have been* | *curious to know* | why I had my umbrella up on such a hot day.'
     | *were obviously* | *wondering* |

1 Look at the three pictures below and decide why the people in them are doing what they are doing. Using the expressions in italics in the example above, make up a similar story for each.

2 Now think up a situation of your own.

▶ How could Harry and James use this language to talk about what happened?

SECTION C: REPORTING

C1   Imagine that Harry or James is telling a friend about what happened. How might they use the following expressions?

tape recorder   to play back
to make out   to pluck up courage
to take one's eyes off   apparently

C2   Now imagine that you are either Harry or James telling a friend about what happened. Write a report, using the language you have practised where you think it is appropriate.

Part two: Expressing the feeling

SECTION A: RECOGNITION

 A1   **Tell me more**

All the remarks below are replies to what someone else has just said. Suggest situations in which they might be said, and what they are replies to.

1 No, no, not at all. Do go on.
2 Oh, yes – very neat, isn't it? Oh – and how do you change the ribbon?
3 Yes, yes, never mind about that – what did *she* say?
4 No, it must have been terrible. Couldn't you get a lift from someone?
5 Yes, my wife and I were just talking about it. You simply must tell me where you got it.
6 Oh yes. I'd been meaning to ask you how you got on.
7 All the same, I can't help wondering whether there isn't more to this Mr Smith than meets the eye.
8 KBK 125F? Are you absolutely sure about that, Miss Whippet?

*"Tell me more about this uncle of yours who smoked forty a
day and lived till he was ninety-seven."*

Which of the remarks, besides expressing interest, also express the following feelings:

impatience   suspicion
surprise   sympathy?

A2 The new face

George works in a large company. Sheila has just been employed as a secretary. On her first day at work, George says to her:

'*So you're the new secretary, are you?*'

On the tape you will hear this remark made in five different ways. In which one is George indicating that:

a) he already knows that she is the new secretary.
b) he has suddenly realised that she is the new secretary.
c) he was expecting someone else to be the new secretary.
d) he thinks that she is an industrial spy.
e) he finds her attractive.

A3 Skeleton in the cupboard

Frank has just met his friend Arthur, whom he has not seen for several years. Last time they met, Arthur had a flourishing hotel business, but since then Frank has heard rumours that things are not going so well. He is curious about the hotel, and cautiously asks Arthur about it.
Read their conversation, choosing the most appropriate expressions for Frank. Give reasons for your choices.

Frank: a) By the way, the hotel's still going, I suppose?
         b) By the way, I don't want to seem inquisitive, but is the hotel still going?
         c) By the way, please tell me if your hotel's still going.
Arthur: Hotel? Oh, that. Oh, I haven't got that any more.
Frank: a) You mean you sold it, don't you?
         b) Oh, you sold it, didn't you.
         c) Oh, so you sold it, did you?
Arthur: Er. . .yes. Yes. I did, actually.
Frank: a) Mm. That's a pity. I wonder why you did that?
         b) Mm. That's a pity. What made you do that, then?
         c) Mm. That's a pity. Tell me why you did that.
Arthur: Well, as a matter of fact, I had to.
Frank: a) Oh, I'm sorry to hear that. Of course, it might've been too expensive to run.
         b) Oh, I'm sorry to hear that. I suppose it was too expensive to run, was it?
Frank: c) Oh, I'm sorry to hear that. Of course, hotels are so expensive to run these days.
Arthur: Er. . .not exactly, no. Oh, by the way. How's Julie getting on?

SECTION B: PRACTICE

B1 The Old Curiosity Shop

Fancy. . .–ing. . .!
Imagine. . .–ing. . .!
I wonder. . .
Do you think. . .?

I bet. . .
I expect. . .
Presumably. . .
They must've. . .

1 Two tourists are looking in the window of The Old Curiosity Shop. They see a Victorian stone hot-water-bottle, and are very interested in it. They begin to speculate about:

a) what it was used for.
b) what kind of people used it.
c) how they used it.
d) how practical it was.
e) how valuable it is.

Suggest things they might say to each other. Use the expressions in the list above.

2 Work in groups or pairs.
There are some other Victorian antiques in the window of The Old Curiosity Shop. Here are some of them. Imagine you are tourists looking in the shop window. You see one of the objects, and are very interested in it. Improvise a conversation about it.

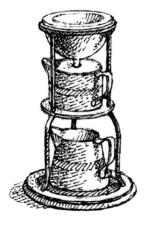

B2   Gossip column

1 Mrs Spice is listening to a fascinating story. This is what she says:

'. . .Uh huh. . .Go on. . .
And what happened then?. . .
But you still haven't told
me about the son. . .
And did she find them?. . .
Whatever did he do then?. . .
And the father?
Now that *is* interesting!. . .'

What kind of story do you think the other person is telling? What is it about?

2 a) In pairs, make up an interesting piece of gossip.
   b) Form new pairs.
   c) Student A: Tell your piece of gossip to B.
       Student B: Interrupt A now and again to show that you are fascinated by the
                   story.

B3   Between strangers

Here are some ways of asking strangers questions when you want to find something
out. They are all used at the *beginning* of conversations.

Excuse me. Could you tell me. . .
Excuse me. Do you happen to know. . .?
Excuse me. I don't want to seem inquisitive, but. . .?
Excuse me. I wonder if you could tell me. . .?
Excuse me. I hope you don't mind me asking, but. . .?
Excuse me. I don't suppose you know. . ., do you?
Excuse me. Do you think you could tell me. . .?
Excuse me. I hope you don't think I'm being inquisitive, but. . .?

1 Which of them would you use if you saw:
   a) an interesting looking building and asked a passer-by what it was?
   b) an Indian woman with a spot painted on her forehead and asked her what it meant?

2 Now look at the situations below and use an appropriate expression to ask a question:

a) You hear two people speaking a foreign language you don't recognise in a restaurant, and you ask one of them what language it is.

b) You see someone wearing a very unusual coat in a pub, and you ask where he/she got it.

c) During you first visit to England, you walk past Hyde Park Corner and see a man standing on a box surrounded by a crowd of people. You wonder what's going on, so you ask one of the crowd.

d) You're standing at a bus stop in England, and see the words QUEUE OTHER SIDE written on it. You're not sure what this means, so you ask one of the people at the bus stop.

e) You're on a train in a foreign country, and you pass an enormous factory. You wonder what it produces, and ask the person sitting opposite you.

f) You see a man digging a hole in the middle of a field, and you ask him why.

3 Work in pairs.

a) Choose one of the more personal situations above, and improvise the conversation that might take place. As the conversation develops, try to use some of the other expressions you have practised in this unit.

b) Choose one of the less personal situations, and improvise a similar conversation.

SECTION C: FREE EXPRESSION

C1 Touchy subject

Work in pairs.

Pair A: You are meeting an acquaintance who you haven't seen for a long time. Last time you met, he had a promising job as a journalist with a large national newspaper. You've heard rumours that he got the sack and is now working part-time for a small local newspaper, but you're not sure.

You want to find out what happened, but you don't want to seem too obviously inquisitive, because you don't want to hurt his feelings.

Work out what you will say to him. Use appropriate expressions from 'Skeleton in the cupboard' (page 87) to help you.

Pair B: You are meeting an acquaintance who you haven't seen for a long time. Last time you met, you had a promising job as a journalist with a large national newspaper. A few months later you did something terrible. You were given the sack, and are now working part-time for a small local newspaper.

You are embarrassed about what happened. You don't really want your acquaintance to know about it, but you think he may already have heard rumours about it.

Decide why you got the sack. Work out what you will say if A asks you about it. Be as evasive as possible, without actually telling lies. Use appropriate expressions from 'Skeleton in the cupboard' (page 87) to help you.

Now form new pairs and improvise the conversation.

C2 **What on Earth?**

Two Martians have arrived on Earth near a lonely farmhouse. The people living there run away and the Martians go inside. They've never visited Earth before, and so they're very interested in everything they see.

A: . . .and I suppose that round thing's a hat.
B: Oh yes. I expect it is.
A: And this long black bit. . .
B: Well, presumably they use that to take it off with.
A: Ah yes. That's rather clever. Here – try it on.
B: Ooh. It's a bit hard, isn't it? Fancy having a hat made of metal.
A: Extraordinary people, these Earthmen. . .

1 What do you think they're looking at?
2 In pairs or groups, write a similar dialogue between the two Martians as they look at another object in the farmhouse. Give enough clues (but not too many) so that it is possible to guess from the conversation what the object is.

Unit 11 Uncertainty

Part one: Talking about the feeling

SECTION A: LISTENING AND DISCUSSION

A1 *Karl:* Er. . .I'm not quite sure about number 5. Should it be 'people' or 'the people'?

Ernest: Well, Karl, just remember the rule – it all depends on whether you're thinking of them as a particular class of people – like 'the cows in that field' – or whether you mean people in England in general, as it were, that is, not all the people but just some of them – like 'cows produce milk'. . .

Karl: So. . .er, do you mean it's 'the people' because it means all the people who drink tea?

Ernest: Er. . .no, because in this case you're thinking of some of these people forming a special class of people. . .or, rather, they're not forming a special class of people. So obviously in this case the answer's 'the people'. Is that clearer now?

Karl: Um. . .

Ernest: Good. Any other problems?

A2 Facts

Discuss these questions.

1 Who are Karl and Ernest?
2 Where do you think they are?
3 What has Karl been doing?
4 What is 'number 5'?
5 What does Ernest try to do?
6 Why does Karl say 'Um'?

A3 Language

Choose the best answers, and justify your choices. More than one answer may be right in each case.

1 Karl . . . . . . number 5.
   a) isn't sure about
   b) isn't certain about
   c) is puzzled by
   d) is baffled by

2 Karl. . . . . . . what to put for number 5.
   a) can't determine
   b) can't decide
   c) can't come to a decision
   d) can't make up his mind

3 Ernest tries to . . . . . . the difference between 'people' and 'the people'.
   a) explain
   b) explain Karl
   c) explain to Karl

4 His explanation is very . . . . . .
   a) complex.
   b) explicit.
   c) complicated.
   d) detailed.

5 Karl can't . . . . . . what Ernest is talking about.
   a) realise
   b) understand
   c) know
   d) make out

6 Karl is completely . . . . . . by Ernest's explanation.
   a) puzzled
   b) baffled
   c) confused
   d) disturbed

7 As he tries to explain, Ernest gets . . . . . .
   a) puzzled.
   b) baffled.
   c) confused.
   d) mixed up.

SECTION B: PRACTICE

B1 In the dark

Albert, the caretaker, saw a light on in the office one night. He was *puzzled*: 'That's odd', he thought. 'I thought I'd turned all the lights off.'

He went inside and found that the safe had been burgled. When the police arrived, they found that all the doors and windows had been securely locked. They were *baffled*: 'We have no idea at all how the burglar could have got in or out', they said.

They questioned Albert for several hours. They asked him the same questions again and again. By the end, Albert was completely *confused*: 'They've asked me so many questions that I can't think straight any more', he said.

Say whether the people in the following situations are *puzzled, baffled,* or *confused*.

1 Ed stared blankly at the maths problem in front of him. He didn't even know how to begin.
2 Ian got a birthday card signed 'From Amelia'. He didn't know anyone of that name, and wondered who she was.
3 Mr Jarvis didn't know how to invest his savings. He'd asked several experts about it, and they'd all given him different advice.
4 When Helen's alarm clock went off, she saw that it was only 4 o'clock in the morning.
5 Janet had learnt so many battles and so many dates that she could no longer remember which date went with which battle.
6 Superficially the inscription looked like Latin, but none of the experts were able to make any sense of it at all.
7 After trying to put the engine back together again all day, Ted gave up.

▶ How could Karl and Ernest use this language to talk about what happened?

B2   Shades of meaning

Can't make out: This is used especially for seeing, hearing and understanding.
e.g. 'The man's face in this photo is blurred. I *can't make out* who it is.'
      'I *couldn't make out* why she was getting so upset.'

Can't work out: This is used especially for solving problems and making calculations.
e.g. 'I *can't work out* how much money I owe him.'
      'I *couldn't work out* why they were digging a hole in the road.'

Can't tell: This is used especially for identifying things and distinguishing things.
e.g. 'I *couldn't tell* when the letter had been posted. There was no postmark.'
      'Alice and Celia are so much alike, I *can never tell* which is which.'

Now talk about the following people, using *make out, work out* or *tell.*

1 Jock: 'So if he has 7 horses, and he divides them equally among his three
        sons. . .Oh, I don't know!'
2 Elspeth: 'What was that? Could you speak a bit more clearly? It's a very bad line.'
3 Harold: 'Margarine or butter? I really don't know. It could be either.'
4 Margery: 'That man's been standing outside our house for three hours now. I
        wonder what he's doing there?'
5 Fiona: 'Oh, it could be any new town anywhere in the world – they all look alike.'

▶ How could Karl and Ernest use this language to talk about what happened?

SECTION C: REPORTING

C1   Imagine that either Karl or Ernest is telling someone about what happened. How
       might they use the following expressions?

       article
       to clarify
       long-winded
       to go on about
       to get the point
       to make head or tail of

C2   Now imagine that you are either a) Karl, telling an English friend about what
       happened, or b) Ernest, telling a colleague about what happened. Write a report,
       using the language you have practised where you think it is appropriate.

Part two: Expressing the feeling

SECTION A: RECOGNITION

A1 Muddled minds

Look at the remarks below and suggest situations in which they are appropriate.

1 Ah, yes, Mr. . .er. . .Oakhill, um. . .Ashburn; you wanted to discuss your son's progress. . .your daughter's progress, that is. . .Mr Firbank, yes of course. . .
2 Hard to tell, really – it could be a plesiosaur. . .unless it's a large fish, of course.
3 But we only had them read last week. Are you sure you're from the Electricity Board?
4 It's like this, Collins. . .How can I put it?. . .The fact is, well, things aren't going too well and there are certain. . .um. . .economies we're going to have to make. . .
5 9 Down, 'Mixed up heads in the Underworld.' Hmm. Must be an anagram. Ah – 'Hades'. . .or is it 'shade'?
6 The thing is, when it says 'teaspoonful', does it mean level or heaped?
7 Wait a minute – you *are* the new secretary, aren't you?

A2 Mental block

Read this conversation and choose the most appropriate remarks for B. Give reasons
for your choices.

A: Oh, yes – Eddie's in town. You remember Eddie, don't you?
B: a) Er. . .Yes, I think I do, actually.
 b) Er. . .No, I think I don't, actually.
 c) Er. . .No, I don't think I do, actually.
A: You know – Eddie Grey! Richard's brother!
B: a) Richard's brother? That's funny. I think Richard's brother's called Alf.
 b) Richard's brother? That's funny. I thought Richard's brother was called Alf.
 c) Richard's brother? That's funny. I was thinking Richard's brother was called
 Alf.
A: No, Alf's Johnny's brother – you remember, Johnny married Joan, Gloria's
 cousin, who. . .
B: a) Now hang on a minute. You're a bit confusing.
 b) Now hang on a minute. You're causing me a bit of confusion.
 c) Now hang on a minute. You're getting me a bit confused.
A: Well, look – Eddie's the one who went to Denmark last year, you know. . .
B: a) Denmark? But surely that was Michael, Sam's brother.
 b) Denmark? But that was certainly Michael, Sam's brother.
 c) Denmark? But of course that was Michael, Sam's brother.
A: No, no, no! Michael's Jane's brother. Now Eddie. . .

A3 Ambivalent answers

Look at the answers below and decide a) what the question might have been;
b) which expresses the most uncertainty, and which the least uncertainty.

1 Um – let me see – Byron, I think.
2 Um, it might be Byron – unless it's Shelley, or Keats. . .someone like that,
 anyway.
3 Byron – at least, I think it is. I'm not absolutely sure, mind you.
4 Hmm, I'm not sure actually. I have a feeling it's Byron, but I may be wrong.

SECTION B: PRACTICE

B1 Unusual angles

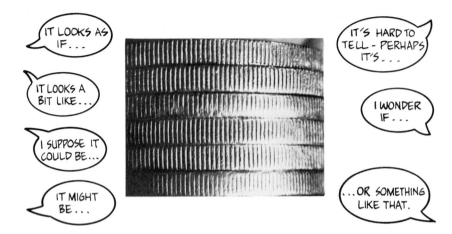

Work in pairs.

1 Look at the photograph above and try to decide what it's a picture of. Use the expressions in the bubbles to help you.

Notice also these expressions, which can be used if you change your mind:

. . .no, wait a minute. . .
. . .but on the other hand. . .
. . .except that. . .
. . .but then again. . .
. . .no, it's too. . .to be a. . .

2 Now choose one of these photographs, and discuss it in the same way:

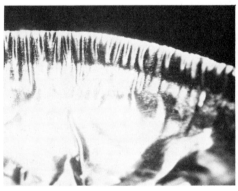 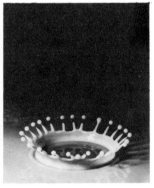 

B2 Alibi

'Well, let's see, I got home from work – oh, it must have been about five o'clock. . .Well, I think it was. It might have been a bit later, I suppose. . .As far as I remember, I just had tea and watched TV for the rest of the evening. . .Ooh, I'm quite sure. Some American detective thing, I think – unless that was Tuesday. . .I don't think so, no. I suppose I might've gone out for some cigarettes, though. . .I really couldn't tell you, I'm afraid. About 10 or so, I should think. . .Mm. I've a feeling it may have been my blue coat and – oh, I really can't remember. . .'

1 a) What questions do you think this person is being asked?
  b) Which of the expressions in the replies indicate that he/she is uncertain?
  c) In pairs, act out the conversation.

2 Work in pairs.
   Student A: Try to find out in as much detail as you can exactly what B was doing over the last 24 hours.
   Student B: Answer A's questions as well as you can.

B3 At a loss

Amy has invited lots of people to a party on Saturday, and she's suddenly realised that her flat's much too small for them.

Amy: The thing is, | I've no idea / I haven't the least idea / I haven't the faintest idea | where I'm going to put them all.

Bob: Hmm. | Why don't you . . . . . . / Have you thought of . . . . . .? |

Amy: Hmm. I could do, I suppose, but . . . . . .

Bob: Oh, ... Well, | you could always . . . . . . / you might try . . . . . . / another possibility would be to . . . . . . |

Amy: | Oh, I couldn't do that – . . . . . . / Oh, that wouldn't be any good – . . . . . . / Yes, I'd thought of that, but . . . . . . |

Bob: Oh, well, I don't know what to suggest, then.

Amy: Unless perhaps . . . . . .

1 a) What suggestions might Bob make?
  b) How might Amy reply?
  c) How might the conversation continue?
  d) In pairs, improvise the conversation. Continue in any way you like.

2 Work in pairs.
   Later in the week Amy has other problems. Choose one of them, and improvise a similar conversation between Amy and Bob.
   a) She has just heard that Aunt Freda is coming to stay the next day, and doesn't know what to do with her.
   b) She wants to buy a new dress for the party, and finds she hasn't enough money.
   c) She has no plans for the evening, and can't think of anything to do.

SECTION C: FREE EXPRESSION

C1 Images

Look at this picture by the surrealist painter Magritte.

In groups, discuss:
a) what it's a picture of.
b) whether the picture has any symbolic meaning.
c) what, if anything, individual parts of the picture symbolise.
d) what title you would give it.

C2 Labour-saving devices

Here are some very useful machines:

a) a machine for looking after your cat when you go away
b) a machine for making pancakes
c) a machine for making your bed
d) a machine that forces you (gently) to get up in the morning, however tired you are
e) a machine to wash your hair

Work in groups.

1 'Invent' one of the machines. Work out in as much detail as possible what the machine would do, what it would look like, and how it would work.
2 Explain your machine to another group. Try to answer any questions they might put to you about it.

Anti-Litter Machine

Unit 12 Sympathy and lack of sympathy

Part one: Talking about the feeling

SECTION A: LISTENING AND DISCUSSION

A1 *Mark:* *Well, luckily, it wasn't worth much anyway. But they absolutely ruined the carpet, and they smashed the window to get in.*
Tony: *Mmm.*
Mark: *Well – it'll cost me pounds to repair all the damage, you know.*
Tony: *Uh huh.*
Mark: *Well, I must say, you don't seem to. . . Tony, is something the matter?*
Tony: *See for yourself.*
Mark: *. . . Tony! Your hi–fi!*
Tony: *And my violin, and the Lowry, and all my first editions. . .*
Mark: *Oh, Tony, I am sorry. How awful for you. It never occurred to me. . .Oh, what a dreadful thing to happen.*

A2 Facts

Discuss these questions.

1 What is the relationship between Mark and Tony?
2 Where are they?
3 What has happened to Mark?
4 Why does Mark ask Tony if something is the matter?
5 What has happened to Tony?
6 What is Tony doing when he says 'See for yourself'?
7 How might Mark's remark 'It never occurred to me. . .' continue?

A3 Language

Choose the best answers and justify your choices. More than one answer may be right in each case.

1 At first, Mark is so . . . . . . with his own problem that he doesn't notice that anything's wrong.
   a) occupied   d) taken
   b) preoccupied   e) taken up
   c) busy

2 When Mark tells Tony about his problem, Tony is . . . . . .
   a) unsympathetic.   c) disinterested.
   b) uninterested.   d) indifferent.

3 Tony doesn't seem to . . . . . . what happened to Mark.
   a) care about   c) take care of
   b) care for

4 Tony's house has been . . . . . .
   a) stolen.   c) robbed.
   b) burgled.

5 Tony is feeling . . . . . .
   a) depressed.   d) upset.
   b) disappointed.   e) miserable.
   c) disillusioned.

6 Mark is . . . . . . when he realises what has happened to Tony.
   a) horrified   c) shocked
   b) terrified

7 When he realises what has happened, Mark is . . . . . .
   a) very sympathetic.   c) very sympathising.
   b) full of sympathy.

SECTION B: PRACTICE

B1 Fellow Feeling

1 Dudley's girlfriend Angie left him yesterday. He told three of his friends about it.

   Donald said: 'Oh dear. I *am* sorry to hear that. You must be feeling terrible.'
   David said: 'Uh huh?'
   Danny said: 'I don't blame her, the way you treated her.'

Later, Dudley commented:

a) He wasn't very sympathetic when I told him.
b) He was most unsympathetic when I told him.
c) He seemed completely indifferent when I told him.

d) He was most sympathetic when I told him.
e) He was full of sympathy when I told him.
f) He wasn't in the least sympathetic when I told him.

Which of these comments did he make about which of his friends?

2 Frank has been injured in a fight. This is how some of his friends reacted when he told them about it:
  a) Hugh: 'Well, it's your own fault, you know. You shouldn't have called him a liar.'
  b) Michelle: 'Oh, did you? Hard luck.'
  c) Joan: 'Oh, how terrible for you. I do hope you get over it soon.'
  d) Timothy: 'What a dreadful thing to happen. Can I help at all?'
  e) Ella: 'Oh yes?'
  f) Gerald: 'Trust you to do a thing like that. That'll teach you to get drunk.'
  g) Yvonne: 'Oh dear, you poor thing. Still, I expect you were partly to blame.'

How might Frank talk about their reactions, using the words: *sympathy, sympathetic, unsympathetic, indifferent*?

▶ How could Mark and Tony use this language to talk about what happened?

B2 Story line

Look at the example and then write similar reports for the situations below. Use the expressions in italics in your answers.

Example
Joyce has just had a car accident. Mary has a stomach ache and tells Joyce all about it.

Joyce: I was feeling *really* $\left|\begin{array}{l}\textit{depressed}\\\textit{upset}\end{array}\right|$ after the accident. Mary came in and *started*

$\left|\begin{array}{l}\textit{going on about}\\\textit{telling me all about}\end{array}\right|$ her stomach ache. She obviously $\left|\begin{array}{l}\textit{had no idea}\\\textit{didn't realise}\end{array}\right|$ that I'd just

had a serious accident. Anyway, I was *so* $\left|\begin{array}{l}\textit{preoccupied}\\\textit{taken up}\end{array}\right|$ with my car insurance

that I'm afraid I $\left|\begin{array}{l}\textit{couldn't concentrate on}\\\textit{couldn't really take in}\end{array}\right|$ what she was saying.

Mary: I started telling Joyce about my stomach ache, but she $\left|\begin{array}{l}\textit{didn't seem to care at all.}\\\textit{seemed completely indifferent.}\end{array}\right|$. In fact, she just sat there and $\left|\begin{array}{l}\textit{ignored}\\\textit{took no notice of}\end{array}\right|$ what I was saying about my visit to the doctor. Then *I noticed that* her foot was in plaster, and $\left|\begin{array}{l}\textit{it suddenly dawned on me}\\\textit{I suddenly realised}\end{array}\right|$ *that* she *must have* had an accident.

1 Alf's wife has just left him a note saying she has run away with the milkman. Raymond has just had an argument with his wife and tells Alf all about it.
2 Sheila has just been given an enormous pile of files to work through – it'll take up

her whole weekend. Rosemary has to work an hour's overtime tonight, and tells Sheila all about it.

3 Bill has just been expelled from school, and is packing his bags. Alistair has just been given some extra homework, and tells Bill all about it.

▶ How could Mark and Tony use this language to talk about what happened?

SECTION C: REPORTING

C1 Imagine that Mark or Tony is telling a friend about what happened. How might they use the following expressions?

to break into   to occur to
to show interest   apologetic
to mumble   embarrassed

C2 Now imagine that you are either a) Mark or b) Tony, telling a friend about what happened. Write a report, using the language you have practised where you think it is appropriate.

Part two: Expressing the feeling

SECTION A: RECOGNITION

"He shouldn't have tried to blow them all out."

 A1 Cause for concern

Look at the remarks below, say whether they express sympathy or not, and suggest situations in which they might be said.

1 Oh, I don't know – it's not as if they weren't insured.
2 Oh, bad luck. It's terribly difficult in this cross-wind, isn't it?
3 Well, it was your idea to go in for it.
4 Please accept my deepest sympathies.

5 Even so, he didn't deserve that long.
6 Poor man. He's got quite enough trouble as it is, without it being all over the front pages.
7 They're adorable, aren't they – pity they taste so good.
8 Aaah, lost your little piggy-wiggy, have you? There, there.

A2 A friend in need

Look at these reassuring remarks and
a) match each remark with the feelings of the person being spoken to;
b) decide what each remark might be a reply to.

1 Never mind. I'm sure we'll find somewhere else.	*impatient*
2 Cheer up. I'm sure they'll turn out to be very nice people.	*annoyed*
3 Take it easy. I'm sure he didn't do it on purpose.	*depressed*
4 Never mind. I'm sure you'll feel better after a few days' holiday	*guilty*
5 Cheer up. I'm sure you did everything you could.	*disappointed*
6 Take it easy. I'm sure we'll get served eventually.	*worried*

A3 Heart of stone

Mr Stone is completely indifferent to everybody else's problems. Here are some of the things he often says:

Search me.
It's no concern of mine.
There's nothing I can do about it.
How should I know?
It's none of my business.
You've only yourself to blame.
Don't ask me.
Serves you right.
It's nothing to do with me.
I'm not surprised.
Haven't a clue.
It's your own fault.

Which four of these remarks do you think Mr Stone is most likely to make in reply to:

a) Hey, did you see that? That man just walked off with a bottle of whisky without paying.
b) I suppose you don't know where the whisky is, do you?
c) Ooh. I've got a terrible hangover from that whisky.

SECTION B: PRACTICE

B1 For and against

A few years ago, Alfred bought a house, and now he can't sell it again.

1 Think of possible reasons why Alfred can't sell his house.
2 Using the expressions above, say
   a) how the sympathetic person might reply
   b) how the unsympathetic person might reply.
3 Work in pairs.
   Make up similar two-line conversations about the situations listed below.
   Either A regrets what he's done and B is sympathetic, *or* A feels sorry for himself and B is unsympathetic.

   a) A is in hospital after a car accident.
   b) A's new boat has sprung a leak.
   c) Someone broke into A's house and stole all his money.
   d) A bought a baby alligator as a pet, and it's growing rather fast.
   e) A has bronchitis.
   f) A had an awful holiday on the Mediterranean.
   g) A's new jeans have split.

B2 Hard luck story

'. . .Oh, I *am* sorry to hear that. How did it happen?. . . It must have been terrible. I hope it's not too painful. . . Oh dear. You must be feeling awful. Still, it's a good thing you've got Doreen to look after you. . .Oh no! Not her as well! The poor girl. . .It would have to happen now, wouldn't it? I hope she'll be all right by Saturday. . .Oh, that *is* a shame. They'll give her another chance, though, won't they?. . .Won't they? Oh, that *is* bad luck! Look, if there's anything I can do to help. . .'

1 a) What do you think the other person is saying?
    b) In pairs, act out the conversation.
2 Work in pairs.
    a) Make up your own hard luck story.
    b) Form new pairs.
       Student A: Tell your hard luck story to B.
       Student B: Sympathise with A.

B3 Other people's problems

Tom works in a factory which operates twenty-four hours a day. His friend Simon has just heard that he has to work on the night shift for the next three months.

Simon: Poor old Tom. Apparently . . . . . .

             I do feel sorry for him.
             He must be terribly . . . . . . about it.
             He must be feeling . . . . . .

Donald: Oh, I don't know –

He hasn't got much to complain about.
He's not so badly off.
It's not all that bad.
It could be worse.

             After all . .

Simon: Oh, come on.

How would you like . . . . . .?
It can't be much fun . . . . . .
It's no joke. . . . . .
I'm sure you wouldn't like. . . . . .

Donald: . . . . . .

1 a) Complete Simon's and Donald's remarks.
   b) How do you think the conversation might continue?
   c) In pairs, act out the conversation between Simon and Donald. Continue in any way you like.

2 Work in pairs.
   Simon has heard three other pieces of bad news. Choose one of them and improvise a similar conversation.
   a) Bernard has just been rushed off to hospital to have his appendix taken out.
   b) Stuart and Lyn have been evicted from their flat.
   c) Maureen's husband is going away for six months on business.

SECTION C: FREE EXPRESSION

C1 Schools of thought

'Children must go to school' warns judge

Unemployed teachers Ken and Hilary Griffiths were warned in court today that they must send their three children to school or face prosecution. The Griffiths, of Birkgate Road, Manwick, had decided to educate the children, aged 6, 8, and 9, themselves, rather than send them to the local primary school. For more than a year they had ignored warnings from the local education authority about their children's absence from class. Asked afterwards whether he would obey the order, Mr Griffiths said 'It looks as if we'll have to now. But we still believe that parents should have the right to bring up their own children if they are qualified teachers.' Mrs Griffiths added 'We have nothing against the local school. It's just that we feel we're in a better position to give our children the kind of education they need.'

Work in groups of five.
Group A: You are a reporter. In an interview for local radio you ask four people whether they sympathise with the Griffiths or not.
Group B: You are a teacher.
Group C: You are a parent.
Group D: You are a policeman.
Group E: You are a student of education.

1 In your groups, work out what you will say in the interview.
2 Form new groups and improvise the interview.

C2 Problem page

Here is the answer to a problem letter written to a popular magazine.

> *Dear Tongue-tied,*
> *I know how you must feel. It's so frustrating when you feel something strongly and you just can't find the words to express it — especially when you're with someone you feel so close to.*
> *It seems to me that your real problem is not that you can't find the right words, but that you're afraid of revealing what you're really like. Try as hard as you can to overcome this fear. Take a few risks. If she really loves you, she won't laugh at you. She'll respect you all the more for showing your true feelings ...*

1 What do you think Tongue-tied wrote in his letter to the Problem Page?
2 Work in groups.
   a) Think of a problem. Write a letter about it to the Problem Page.
   b) Pass it to another group.
   c) Write a sympathetic answer to the letter you have received.

ppendix   Adjectives and verbs used to describe feelings

This table shows:
1 what prepositions to use with adjectives that describe feelings;
2 equivalent verbs and adjectives that describe what *causes* the feeling.

Example

I	felt / was	annoyed	about it. / with him.	He / It	annoyed me.	I found	him / it	annoying.

* amazed by/to (hear) (8)	to amaze	amazing
angry about something/with someone (7)	(to anger)	—
annoyed about something/with someone (5, 7)	to annoy	annoying
anxious about (3)	—	—
anxious to (do) (1)	—	—
* astonished by/to (hear) (8)	to astonish	astonishing
* baffled by (11)	to baffle	baffling
bored by/with (10)	to bore	boring
concerned about (3)	—	—
(*) confused by (11)	to confuse	confusing
* delighted with/to (hear) (6)	to delight	delightful
* desperate to (do) (1)	—	—
disappointed with/by (9)	to disappoint	disappointing
(*) disillusioned with (9)	(to disillusion)	—
dissatisfied with (9)	to dissatisfy	unsatisfactory
eager to (do) (1)	—	—
excited about/by (2)	to excite	exciting
(*) fascinated by (10)	to fascinate	fascinating
frightened by (3)	to frighten	frightening
frustrated by/with (9)	to frustrate	frustrating
furious about something/with someone (7)	to infuriate	infuriating
glad about/to (hear) (6)	—	—
hurt by (7)	to hurt	(hurtful)
impatient with (5)	—	—
impressed by (4)	to impress	impressive
* indifferent to (12)	—	—
indignant about something/with someone (7)	—	—
interested by/in (10)	to interest	interesting
intrigued by (10)	to intrigue	intriguing
irritated by something/with someone (5)	to irritate	irritating
keen to (do) (1)	—	—
moved by (4)	to move	moving
nervous about (3)	—	—
offended by (7)	to offend	offensive
* overwhelmed by (4)	to overwhelm	overwhelming
pleased with/to (hear) (6)	(to please)	(pleasing)

puzzled by (11)	to puzzle	puzzling
relieved to (hear) (6)	—	—
(*) shocked by/to (hear) (8)	to shock	shocking
struck by (4)	(to strike)	striking
surprised by/to (hear) (8)	to surprise	surprising
sympathetic towards someone (12)	—	—
* terrified by (3)	to terrify	terrifying
* thrilled by/with (2)	to thrill	thrilling
unsympathetic towards someone (12)	—	—
worried about (3)	to worry	worrying

Adjectives marked ***** are 'absolutes', i.e. they describe a strong feeling and cannot be used wit 'very', 'slightly', etc.

e.g. I was $\left|\begin{array}{c}slightly\\very\end{array}\right|$ annoyed with him.

    I was *absolutely* furious with him.

Adjectives marked (*****) can be used either as 'absolutes' or as normal adjectives.

Numbers in brackets refer to units in this book.